STRENGTH
Training

Beginners, Bodybuilders, Athletes

PHILIP E. ALLSEN
Brigham Young University

Fifth Edition

KENDALL/HUNT PUBLISHING COMPANY
4050 Westmark Drive · Dubuque, Iowa 52002

Book Team

Chairman and Chief Executive Officer   Mark C. Falb
President and Chief Operating Office   Chad M.Chandlee
Vice President, Higher Education   David L. Tart
Director of National Book Program   Paul B. Carty
Editorial Development Manager   Georgia Botsford
Developmental Editor   Denise M. LaBudda
Assistant Vice President, Production Services   Christine E. O'Brien
Senior Production Editor   Carrie Maro
Permissions Editor   Colleen Zelinsky
Cover Designer   Sandy Beck

Cover images: Main image and lower middle image courtesy PhotoDisc, Inc. Lower left
and right images © Kendall/Hunt Publishing Company, courtesy Ken Smith.

Lineart on pages 51–60 by Spencer Glenn.

Contents

About the Author

Philip E. Allsen is professor of exercise sciences and director of the Fitness for Life program at Brigham Young University in Provo, Utah. Widely known for his expertise in physical fitness, sports medicine, and athletic conditioning, Dr. Allsen has written 22 textbooks and authored more than one hundred articles on the topics of strength and physical fitness. The Fitness for Life program, which he developed at Brigham Young University, now serves approximately seven thousand students at the institution each year and has been adopted by more than four hundred schools in the United States.

Dr. Allsen has served as a conditioning consultant to a large number of professional athletes and professional teams. He is a member of the American College of Sports Medicine; the American Alliance of Health, Physical Education, Recreation and Dance; the National Collegiate Physical Education Association; and the National Strength and Conditioning Association.

In recognition of outstanding achievement and service in the field of strength and conditioning, Dr. Allsen has been inducted into the USA Strength and Conditioning Coaches Hall of Fame.

Preface

Anyone who is interested in increasing their performance, whether in athletics or any other aspect of life, can do so by increasing body strength. *Strength Training: Beginners, Bodybuilders, Athletes* presents strength development programs for beginning strength trainers, for those who wish to improve their athletic ability, and for those interested in becoming serious bodybuilders.

I have had the opportunity to supervise strength training programs for thousands of people, ranging from individuals who have never participated in any type of strength program to elite athletes who compete on a professional level. Physique athletes who have been strength trained have gone on to win national contests in bodybuilding.

The first two chapters of this book give the scientific background on the physiological and anatomical changes brought about by engaging in a strength development program. The basic concepts necessary to understand strength programs are also presented in these two chapters.

The remaining chapters deal with the actual design of specific strength training programs. These chapters present many different exercises for each of the particular muscle groups to help readers develop a total and comprehensive training program. Readers may select from among a variety of exercises to strengthen the various body parts. Each exercise is illustrated by pictures that demonstrate correct body position and technique. The pictures are accompanied by explanations of the action, as well as precautions to take. Readers who apply these concepts can easily design programs that are safe and efficient.

Strength training is important for everyone. This type of training can ensure greater productivity in many areas of life, as well as enable practitioners to enjoy the positive benefits of an enhanced self-concept.

Acknowledgments

I would like to extend my sincere thanks to those who took the time to set up, pose for, and photograph all of the new photos in Chapter 5. Stanley Guillaume, Kathleen Pape, Jesse Shekleton, Christopher Phetz, Gary Newsom and Michelle Glasgow spent many hours being posed, moved, and re-posed to get the correct form for each of the exercises. Certified Personal Trainer Traci Cooley not only posed, but was also the consultant during the multiple photo shoots. Ken Smith of Design Photography, Inc. did an excellent job with the photography. I would also like to thank Tom VanGelder and Linda Kelley from Phoenix Fitness in Dubuque, Iowa, for the use of their facilities and equipment, and The Bike Shack of Dubuque, Iowa, for loaning some necessary equipment. Thanks also to Spencer Glenn for the anatomical drawings.

1

Why Train for Strength?

Often when the word *strength* enters into a conversation, people think of men with bulging muscles or NFL football players crashing into one another on the field of battle. People then ask why ordinary individuals should give serious consideration to engaging in a strength training program. Sometimes people make statements such as, "What good will increased strength do for me in my business as a computer programmer?"

To answer these questions and dispel some of the misconceptions surrounding the topic of strength, let us consider what strength is and why strength can give everyone an advantage in participating in the activities of daily life.

STRENGTH AND ITS ADVANTAGES

Strength is defined as the ability to exert force against resistance. Force is the basis of all motion, and when we examine the world we live in, we can easily observe that it is a world of motion. Strength then becomes an important aspect in performing the tasks of daily living, such as lifting, walking, running, doing housework, and engaging in recreational tasks.

Another aspect of movement is *power*. Power is defined as the rate at which energy can be released, or the rate of doing work. The formula for power is as follows:

$$\text{Power} = \text{Force} \times \frac{\text{Displacement in the direction of force}}{\text{Time}}$$

Displacement in the direction of force divided by time equals velocity. Thus, the two factors that influence power are force (strength) and velocity. To affect power, a training program must affect either strength or velocity or, if possible, both of these factors at the same time. Of these two variables, it is much more difficult to bring about changes in velocity than in strength. Thus, the key to developing increased power is the change that a training program can bring about on the development of strength.

Research reveals that a properly designed strength program can also have a positive effect on velocity if the right energy releasing systems are trained in the strength program.

1

In this way, power becomes one of the keys to a more productive life. It is not time itself that is important but rather what takes place in that time; productivity determines the difference between success and failure. By increasing your power output, you can accomplish more work in a shorter period of time.

Consider the practical example of mowing the lawn. If you increase your strength and bring about a greater power output, the work of mowing the lawn can be accomplished much more quickly. A friend gave the following reason for participating in a strength program: "I can finish my yard work in a short period of time, and this allows me to get on the golf course where I can apply force to the golf ball with a great amount of joy!"

The past few years have seen some remarkable performances in athletic achievement. Athletes are jumping farther and higher, runners are breaking records in most of the running events, and swimming records are broken in nearly every large swimming meet.

Physiologically, the body has been operating the same way for a long while, so there must be a reason why the human body is breaking athletic records that were thought to be impossible to change. When we examine the training procedures these record-breaking athletes engage in, we find that one of the greatest causes of improvement is the proper use of a strength training program.

If strength is the ability to exert force and force is a tendency to cause motion, then strength is important not only to the athlete but also to all individuals in everyday life. If more work can be accomplished in a shorter period of time, a person is more powerful. If all else remains equal, an increase in strength will contribute to an improvement in the performance of the human body.

Another reason for engaging in strength training is that it makes you feel better and look better. A person does not have to be a so-called bodybuilder to value how an attractive body can have a positive effect on self-concept. In a survey of the men and women engaged in a series of strength development classes, over 80 percent responded that the major reason for taking the class was that they wished "to look better."

Since many people express a desire to look better, a discussion of body composition is important. The human body is composed of materials that are referred to as *lean body mass* and *fat mass.* Lean body mass is made up primarily of muscle tissue, nervous tissue, connective tissue, bone, and fluids, and fat mass is the fat that the body stores. Many people in our society have an excess amount of body fat, and this leads to the problem of obesity. One estimate is that by the age of fifty, almost 50 percent of the people in the United States are approaching obesity, or overfatness.

The relationship between the amount of muscle mass in the body and excess body fat is often overlooked. The amount and size of muscle decrease in many people as they get older because of a lack of a strength training stimulus. As muscle mass decreases, the person uses less energy even at rest, and a greater percentage of the body weight becomes fat. Fat tissue does not burn nearly as many calories at rest as muscle tissue, and thus the individual continues to gain body fat. In other words, many people become fat because they are using fewer calories as a result of the loss of muscle mass caused by a lack of activity. Since people spend more time in sitting than in any other activity, the average American becomes overfat as he or she grows older.

Ancel Keys, a researcher in weight control, showed that the decrease in caloric expenditure in different age groups at rest was related to the change in muscle mass rather than to age. For example, at age sixty a person will use approximately fifteen calories less per hour than a person who is twenty-six years of age. Over a twenty-four-hour period this would be a total of 360 unused calories per day. If that person wanted to retain the same eating habits but not put on fat, he or she would have to walk approximately six miles each day to expend the 360 calories, since the energy used in walking one mile is about sixty calories. The sixty-year-old individual, therefore, must increase activity, decrease caloric intake, or else put on more fat.

A person can help eliminate the problem of overfatness by using a strength development program to maintain muscle mass so that caloric expenditure at rest won't decrease. Thus a person won't have to exercise so extensively to combat obesity. The body will continue to use more calories if muscle mass is maintained throughout life.

A common misconception about strength development is that a strength training program will cause "muscle-boundness," or a loss of flexibility. Many scientific studies indicate that the opposite is true—that engaging in a strength program correctly will actually bring about an improvement in flexibility. One study, conducted at the Olympic Games, tested the flexibility of the competing athletes and found that the most flexible athletes were the gymnasts, swimmers, and weightlifters.

The key to maintaining good flexibility is to take the body parts through a full range of motion. This can be accomplished by engaging in a proper strength development program. By using correct techniques, you will develop strength throughout the entire range of movement of the body musculature.

The ability of the body to resist the stresses that can result from an injury can be increased by obtaining a greater amount of strength. In the athletic world, statistics indicate that athletic injuries, such as in football, are reduced when teams engage in a strength development program. The fatigue of sports participation combats the body's ability to withstand the disruption of movement, but with an increase in strength, the athlete is more powerful and thus retains the ability to perform in the later stages of the contest. This same advantage is important in performing everyday tasks, such as lifting or carrying objects.

Health Benefits of Strength Training

Besides increasing strength, creating more collagenous fibrils in connective tissue, bringing about changes in nervous tissue, and increasing bone density, a strength training program has other health benefits.

Some of the risk factors for coronary heart disease (CHD) are determined by the variables of blood cholesterol and blood lipids and the transport molecules known as lipid proteins. A total body strength program has a positive effect on these variables.

High blood sugar (glucose) levels and high insulin levels are risk factors for diabetes and CHD. Recent evidence has revealed that strength training can bring about positive changes in glucose metabolism.

Colon cancer is associated with a prolonged gastrointestinal transit time, and sedentary living is associated with an increase of cancer of the colon. An accelerated transit time is associated with a strength training program that develops the abdominal musculature. One study found that strength training brought about an average acceleration of 56 percent in gastrointestinal transit time after thirteen weeks of training.

A strength training program can help an individual release emotional stress. Studies have found a decrease in neuromuscular tension following a strength work-out.

Body image and self-concept are influenced in a positive manner as a person's physical appearance improves due to a proper strength training program.

WOMEN AND STRENGTH TRAINING

Women considering strength training are sometimes concerned that strength exercises will make them appear less feminine. The fear is that training will produce large, unsightly, bulging muscles. In the past few years, research has disputed this myth. Women have the same muscle properties as men, but because of endocrinological differences, they respond to a training stimulus in different ways. Before puberty, there is little difference between the muscular size and strength of boys and girls, but with the onset of puberty, testosterone from the testes of the male and estrogen from the ovaries of the female begin to enter the bloodstream and trigger the development of the appropriate secondary sexual characteristics. The result is that men develop a greater quantity of muscle tissue and respond with a greater gain of muscle mass when they engage in a strength program.

In most cases, women will not gain a large amount of muscle mass when training, but they will obtain increased strength, which will enable them to better perform daily activities. The diameter of a muscle cell can increase as much as 30 percent without measurable growth in the girth of a body limb, so women do not have to worry about increased body size. There is no physiological reason for women not to engage in a strength training program and no need to suggest different training programs on the basis of sex. Both women and men can experience the same general benefits; it is only the degree of gain in muscle tissue that will differ.

An example of this is one of the female models utilized for the strength training exercises on pages 132 to 136. Michelle Glasgow began an Olympic weight training program at the age of 12. She was 16 years of age when these photos were taken and is currently a national and international ranked female Olympic lifter. She is also a member of the ballroom dance team at her high school which is ranked as one of the best in her state. An examination of her photos and other female photos in the exercise section certainly dispels the thought that increased strength detracts from femininity.

STRENGTH TRAINING FOR THOSE OVER FORTY

Some people ask whether those over the age of forty should engage in strength training. The answer is that all the advantages of increased strength hold true for any age.

Research comparing the rate of strength gains in men and women of various ages shows that the rates are similar for all age groups. One study used men and women with an average age of ninety. After strength training for eight weeks in a three-day-per-week program, the subjects experienced a 174 percent increase in strength.

Our youth-oriented society tends to neglect the needs of its older citizens. If you are an individual who falls into the over-forty category, rest assured that engaging in a proper strength development program can not only increase your strength but also increase the overall performance of your body.

STRENGTH TRAINING AND CHILDREN

Another question involves whether strength training is an appropriate activity for children before the age of pubescence. At one time the assumption was that prepubescent boys and girls could not increase strength because of a lack of adult hormones. A large amount of research indicates that this assumption is false and that children can obtain significant strength gains in a properly designed program.

Other research has revealed that a strength training program will also contribute to motor performance gains and other health-related benefits such as injury prevention, improvements in blood lipid profiles, an increase in bone density, and a positive effect on body composition. Strength training also has been found to contribute to a more positive self-concept and body image in children.

The National Strength and Conditioning Association and the American Orthopaedic Society for Sports Medicine have stated that proper strength training will have lasting benefits on young participants. They have suggested the following guidelines in the design of strength programs for this age group:

1. Require a medical examination before participating in the strength program.
2. Make sure the training facility provides a safe exercise environment.
3. Participants should have the emotional maturity to accept and follow proper training directions.
4. Instructors should be qualified and remember the uniqueness of each child.
5. Include warm-up and cool-down exercises in the training program.
6. Demonstrate proper exercise techniques for each exercise utilized in the program.
7. Increase the resistance gradually as strength improves in the participants.
8. Prohibit one repetition maximum lifts during the program to prevent possible injury.
9. Remember that strength training is part of an overall conditioning program.

These guidelines are excellent suggestions not only for children but also for any strength trainer regardless of age.

COMMONLY ASKED QUESTIONS CONCERNING STRENGTH PROGRAMS

Through the years the author has kept track of questions that have been asked about strength training. Following are a list of these questions.

Why is it recommended that a person allow at least one day between strength work-outs? For example, work-out on MWF or TThSat.

All that a training program of any type, such as strength training, does is upset the homeostasis or equilibrium of various body systems. Time must be given for change or accommodation to take place in the systems. An alternate day recovery time contributes to a time for change to take place.

How much strength does an individual need?

Since all individuals are different, there is not an exact answer to this question. Since strength contributes to power (rate of doing work) which is important both in sport and daily activity, an increase in strength will improve the efficiency of body movements.

How can a person determine if they are progressing?

If strength is the major outcome a person wants, then the best indicator of progress is the amount of weight one can lift in the selected strength exercises.

A person who wishes to change their body composition can take various body measurements to indicate positive change.

Appendix A contains Body Measurement Charts and Appendix C provides Strength Training Records to determine strength increases.

How can a person maintain strength once they have achieved a certain amount?

Strength in many cases can be maintained by having a strength work-out once a week. In order to do this, close to maximum resistance must be used for each exercise. A work-out schedule of this type might contribute to muscle soreness.

Can a person obtain strength gains by just doing one set of each strength exercise?

The answer is yes, but research indicates that a multiple-set system will allow a person to obtain training effects much faster. Though a single-set system is not as effective, it can be utilized when a person does not have the time to engage in a multiple-set program.

Are there specific exercises that I can select for specific areas of the body?

In Chapter 5 you will find information to plan a strength training program. It will explain the muscles of the body and list different exercises to train specific body parts.

What is circuit training?

This is a form of training where specific exercises are organized at stations in the training room. A person does a given number of repetitions for a given amount of time and then goes to the next station. The difficulty of each exercise can be increased by reducing the amount of time allotted to complete the required repetitions.

What are anabolic steroids?

Anabolic steroids are synthetic derivatives of the male hormone testosterone. People take them hoping to stimulate increased muscle growth and strength gains. Because of the negative effects of anabolic steroids they have been banned by most sport governing bodies. By going to page 23, you will find more information concerning the use of supplements.

What will happen to my strength if I stop strength training.

The effects of any training program will decrease if the training stimulus is removed. This is one of the reasons that strength training should be a lifelong activity.

Is the muscle tissue in women different from the muscle tissue in men?

The muscle tissue is the same in both genders. Due to hormonal differences men usually have a greater amount of muscle tissue and usually greater total body strength.

Will strength training have a negative effect on flexibility and cause a person to become "muscle-bound"?

Flexibility is defined as the ability to take a joint-lever system through a range of motion and being muscle-bound means the inability to go through a normal range of motion. In a strength training program, if a person uses a full range of motion in the various exercises, the flexibility will increase.

What are isometrics and can this type of training increase strength?

An isometric contraction is a muscle contraction with little or no movement. If the resistance is high enough, it can develop strength. It should be noted that strength gains are specific to any given angle that the resistance is encountered and the rest of the range of motion will not have an increase in strength.

If I stop strength training will my muscle mass turn to fat?

Muscle tissue and fat tissue are different from each other and you cannot turn a muscle cell into a fat cell or vice versa. If the daily caloric intake is over the amount needed to maintain the body, some of the excess calories will contribute to an increase in fat tissue. It should be pointed out that one pound of muscle tissue compared to one pound of fat tissue requires three times more calories at rest. By increasing your muscle mass, you now have a fat-using mechanism that will work to reduce fat 24 hours each day.

Will strength training have a negative effect on coordination for other sports?

No. Many research studies indicate a positive effect. Remember power (how much work you can do in a given amount of time) is what determines success and strength is a major contributor to power.

Is nutrition important in a strength training program?

Yes, Nutrition provides the various systems of the body with substances to repair, maintain, and change in a positive nature. Information about nutrition can be found starting on page 19.

CONCLUSION

An examination of all the ways strength can contribute to the overall efficiency of the human body reveals that a strength development program should be a lifetime process. When you make the decision to start a strength program, you have started a new lifestyle. Maintaining that lifestyle is important, since strength is reversible and will decline if you do not continue to obtain a strength stimulus for your entire life.

2 *Principles and Programs*

MOTOR UNITS

The human body has about 434 muscle groups that are used to move the various parts of the anatomy. Each one of these muscles is made up of what are known as *motor units*. A motor unit is composed of a single motor neuron and all of the muscle cells innervated by this neuron. Figure 2.1 is a diagram of motor units.

All motor units do not have the same capabilities and are classified as either slow-twitch, fast-twitch a, or fast twitch x motor units. Table 2.1 summarizes the characteristics of the various motor units. An individual muscle is composed of both fast-twitch and slow-twitch muscle units. Fast-twitch units have the ability to contract very rapidly and thus generate a large amount of force in a short period of time. They expend their energy sources quickly and thus are more easily fatigued.

Slow-twitch units can exert force for longer periods of time and are used for activities that require submaximum force, such as jogging, walking, and long-distance swimming. Even though genetics determines whether we have muscles composed of a greater percentage of slow-twitch units or fast-twitch units, strength training can affect the ability of both units to exert force.

During the contraction of a muscle, motor unit recruitment is greatly affected by the force necessary to perform the movement. Slow-twitch motor units are usually recruited to lift a light weight. However, in lifting a heavy weight, all of the motor units might have to be recruited. *Ramp effect* refers to the relationship between the percentage of muscle fibers used and the amount of muscular force required to recruit motor units.

One important implication of the ramp effect is how it may affect a strength training program. To increase the potential of all of the motor units, especially the potential of the fast-twitch motor units, the training must be of a fairly high intensity. The use of a proper strength program allows all of the motor units to be stimulated and thus increases their capability to become stronger and exert a greater force.

Figure 2.2 illustrates this idea and also indicates the number of RMs (repetitions maximum) necessary to provide a training effect.

Motor unit type is usually determined in the laboratory by an invasive procedure that involves collecting a small sample of muscle tissue using a needle biopsy. The muscle sample is then chemically analyzed to determine the ratio of various motor units contained in the muscle.

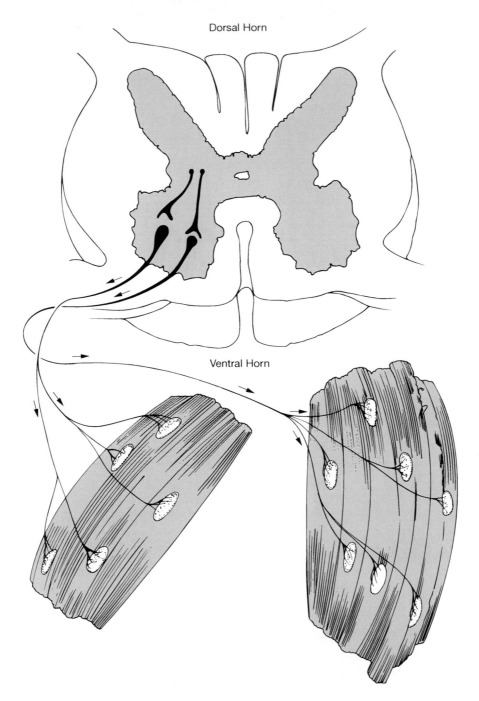

Dorsal Horn

Ventral Horn

Figure 2.1 Motor Units

A field test can be used to obtain a rough estimation of motor unit type within a muscle group. The following procedures are used to estimate motor unit type:

1. Establish a one-repetition maximum (1 RM) for the specific lift.
2. Perform as many repetitions as possible using 80 percent of the 1 RM.
   a. If you can complete only a few repetitions (less than seven), then the muscle group is likely composed of more than 50 percent fast-twitch motor units.
   b. If you can complete many repetitions (more than twelve), then the muscle group likely has more than 50 percent slow-twitch motor units.

Characteristic	ST	FT$_a$	FT$_x$
NEURAL ASPECTS			
Motoneuron size	Small	Large	Large
Motoneuron recruitment threshold	Low	High	High
Motor nerve conduction velocity	Slow	Fast	Fast
STRUCTURAL ASPECTS			
Muscle fiber diameter	Small	Large	Large
Mitochondrial density (aerobic energy)	High	High	Low
Capillary density	High	Medium	Low
Myoglobin (aerobic) density	High	Medium	Low
ENERGY SUBSTRATE			
Creatine phosphate stores	Low	High	High
Glycogen (carbohydrate) stores	Low	High	High
Triglyceride (fat) stores	High	Medium	Low
ENZYMATIC ASPECTS			
Glycolytic (anaerobic) enzyme activity	Low	High	High
Oxidative (aerobic) enzyme activity	High	High	Low
FUNCTIONAL ASPECTS			
Twitch (contraction) time	Slow	Fast	Fast
Relaxation time	Slow	Fast	Fast
Force production	Low	High	High
Fatigue resistance	High	Low	Low
DISTRIBUTION			
Endurance athletes	High	Medium to high	Low
Sprint, explosive athletes	Medium to low	Medium to high	High

Figure 2.2   Ramp Effect and Muscular Force

c. If you can only complete between seven and twelve repetitions, then the muscle group probably has an equal proportion of slow-twitch and fast-twitch muscle units.

JOINT–LEVER SYSTEM

Many times when people think of a strength training program, they only consider changes that take place in the muscle tissue. Movement in the body is produced through the use of joint-lever systems, which are composed of nervous tissue, connective tissue, skeletal tissue, and muscle tissue. A proper strength training program may increase the output of a joint-lever system by bringing about changes in one or more of the various tissues. Figure 2.3 is an example of a joint-lever system.

The exact physiological cause of increased strength is not known, but an examination of research reveals that changes that take place in the joint-lever system might contribute to an increase in strength. An indication of these sites is contained in figure 2.4.

Figure 2.3　Joint–Lever System

Figure 2.4　Changes in the Joint–Lever System

Nervous Tissue

As a result of a strength program, a neural adaptation could bring about an increased neural drive to muscle. This has been indicated by the use of electromyographic (EMG) studies. Other changes in the nervous system may bring about a possible increased synchronization of the motor units that make up the various muscle groups, and this might contribute to increased strength.

Sensory units located in the tendons, known as Golgi tendon organs, when stimulated by tension placed on a joint-lever system, cause a muscle to relax. A strength program may bring about changes that partly inhibit this mechanism and allow a greater force to be produced by the muscle. Much of the increased strength output in the first few weeks of a strength training program is thought to be due to changes in the nervous system.

Connective Tissue

The body uses connective tissue to hold bones and muscles together. Connective tissue is also used to transmit the force of a muscle contraction to the bone or lever arm of the joint-lever system. Very few muscles are directly attached to the bone by muscle alone. The muscle is usually attached to a tendon, which is composed of connective tissue. To transmit the force, the connective tissue relies on many collagenous fibrils, which are primarily composed of protein. Figure 2.5 is a diagram of connective tissue. A proper strength training program increases these fibrils and thus increases the capability of connective tissue to transmit force to the bone.

Skeletal Tissue

Skeletal tissue is used to construct the levers in a joint-lever system. A proper strength training program increases the deposit of mineral salts in the skeletal tissue and thus increases bone density.

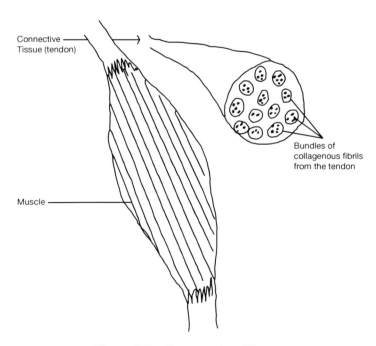

Figure 2.5   Connective Tissue

Osteoporosis is a condition of increased porosity and decreased bone mineral density. More women die each year from problems resulting from hip fractures related to osteoporosis than from the combination of deaths from breast cancer, uterine cancer, and ovarian cancer. Osteoporosis might be prevented if the prevention starts early enough in a person's life. Two major factors that can help to prevent osteoporosis are weight-bearing exercises and a proper diet with adequate calcium. Adolescent boys and girls should have a daily intake of at least 1,200 milligrams of calcium, and adults should take in at least 1,000 milligrams per day. After menopause, women should have a daily intake of at least 1,500 milligrams per day.

Regular weight-bearing exercise will help prevent osteoporosis. Increasing the amount of resistance, such as in strength training, may provide the body with an effective stimulus to cause an increase in the density of the bone. Research reveals that the forces produced on certain bones, such as the lumbar vertebrae in the back, during walking and jogging are 1.75 times the body's weight. During a strength training program using weights, the loads may be as much as 5 to 6 times the body's weight. Thus, the results of a strength training program have beneficial effects on skeletal tissue.

Muscle Tissue

Because of its ability to contract, muscle tissue is the only tissue in the body that has the capability to produce a force. Figure 2.6 contains a diagram of the components of a muscle cell.

Figure 2.6   Muscle Cell

A muscle is made up of many muscle cells known as motor units. To increase the strength of the muscle, usually an increase in the size of the muscle must occur. *Hypertrophy, hyperplasia,* and *atrophy* are terms that are useful in understanding how a muscle might become larger or smaller:

Hypertrophy: Increase in cell size

Hyperplasia: Increase in number of cells

Atrophy: Decrease in cell size and/or a decrease in cell number

Research indicates that the major change in muscle tissue as a result of a strength training program is due to hypertrophy of the muscle cells.

An examination of figure 2.6 reveals that a muscle cell is made up of bundles called myofibrils. Myofibrils contain the contractile filaments that allow the muscle cell to contract. The stimulus of a strength training program appears to release chemical modulators that cause the myofibrils to split and activate chemical mechanisms that increase the amount of contractile filaments within the myofibrils. This increased mass allows the cell to exert a greater force and become stronger.

Muscles can also become weaker through the process of atrophy, which is a decrease in the size of a cell due to loss of myofibrils and contractile filaments. Atrophy also refers to a loss of muscle cells. As explained earlier, a muscle is composed of motor units that are classified as slow-twitch, fast-twitch a, and fast-twitch x motor units. To stimulate or overload the fast-twitch motor units, you must utilize relatively high resistance. If these motor units are not used, they begin to atrophy. The fast-twitch motor units are highly susceptible to atrophy, especially after the age of twenty-five. Once these cells are lost, the body cannot restore them. This is one of the reasons why strength training should be a lifelong activity.

WEAKEST JOINT ANGLE PRINCIPLE

As a joint-lever system goes through a full range of motion, the ability to exert force at different joint angles changes. Figure 2.7 illustrates this concept.

A muscle exerts the greatest force when it is in a slightly stretched position. Another factor that affects the production of force is the mechanical alignment of the bones that make up the lever arms. This factor is referred to as *mechanical advantage,* or the ratio of the force arm to the resistance arm. For example, the most advantageous joint angle during arm flexion, using the biceps, is thought to be approximately when the elbow is flexed at a 100° angle. Thus when a joint-lever system is working through a range of motion, the variables of muscle length and mechanical advantage are going to have an effect on the force produced by the system.

Some machines supposedly have the capability to apply maximum resistance at every joint angle through a range of motion. This might appear to be an advantage, as shown in figure 2.8. These machines are known as *accommodating resistance machines* and are based on the principle of using either isokinetic or variable resistance. In real-life movements, however, using the joint-lever systems of the body through a full range of motion, the system will always be limited by the weakest joint angle.

Regardless of the training method chosen, the overload principle, discussed next, must be utilized to obtain strength gains, and the resistance must be progressively increased as the muscles increase in strength.

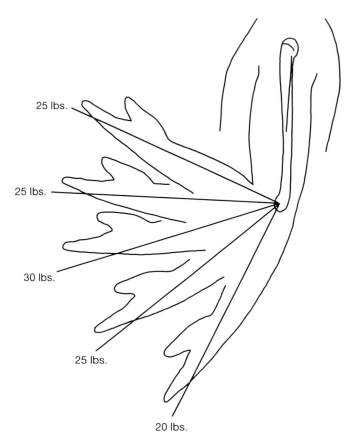

Figure 2.7 Change of Ability to Exert Force Through a Range of Motion

OVERLOAD PRINCIPLE

In any physical fitness program, the *overload principle* refers to the requirements necessary to bring about improvement in the various systems of the body. As the body is subjected to loads greater than those to which the systems are accustomed, the various systems adjust and increase their capacity to perform physical work.

A classic example concerns the Greek hero Milo of Crotona. Each day Milo lifted a calf to his shoulders and ran through the stables. As the calf grew and added body weight, the increased weight provided the overload necessary to bring about the physiological changes in Milo's body systems to make him stronger. The same principle accounts for increased strength in any training program.

One contemporary example demonstrating the overload principle is the jogger who first runs only one mile and then each week adds another mile to the training program. Because of this overload, certain systems of the body are stimulated and increase their ability to perform the work of jogging. In time the jogger will easily be able to cover ten or more miles on a training run.

Specific body systems require specific overloads. In jogging, for instance, the cardiovascular system requires an overload that is different from the overload necessary to bring about strength gains. This is referred to as the *law of specificity*. The minimum resistance that a person can use and still be confident of obtaining strength gains is approximately 60 percent of the maximum force (1 RM) that a muscle group can exert. The following chapters contain all of the information necessary to ensure that the specific overload for strength will be contained in the planning of a strength training program.

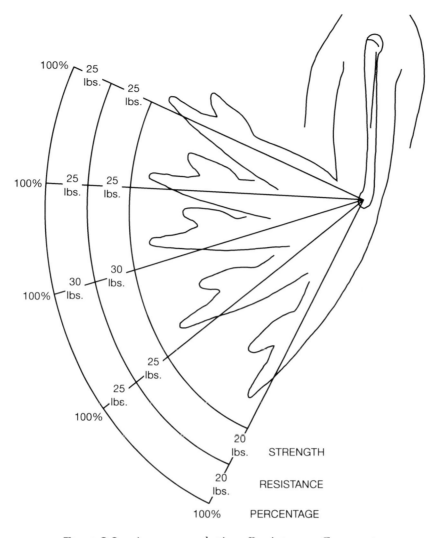

Figure 2.8 Accommodating Resistance Concept

BASIC DEFINITIONS

Before organizing a strength program, familiarity with the following definitions is necessary:

Accommodating resistance: the use of a machine that adjusts the resistance in an attempt to obtain maximum resistance through a full range of motion

Barbell: a bar with iron plates attached

Bodybuilder: a person who uses weight training to obtain a more muscular physique; a physique athlete

Concentric action: a shortening of the muscle against resistance

Dumbbell: a hand weight

Dynamic action: muscle action with movement

Eccentric action: a lengthening of the muscle against resistance

Free weights: barbells and dumbbells; free weights differ from strength training machines, which are restricted on how they can be used

Isokinetic training: the use of a machine that controls the speed of a muscle contraction and attempts to vary the resistance according to the muscle force applied

Isometric action: muscle action without movement

Muscular endurance: the ability to perform repeated muscle movements for a given period of time

Periodization: dividing the training year into periods and manipulating the stress of training to combat over-training

Physique: the body structure; organization or development of the physical appearance

Progressive resistance training: increasing the amount of weight lifted as one becomes stronger

Recovery period: the rest interval time between sets

Repetition maximum: the maximum amount of weight lifted for a given number of repetitions. For example, 1 RM would be the maximum weight lifted for one repetition, and 6 RM would be the maximum weight lifted for six repetitions

Repetitions: the number of times an exercise is performed

Set: a given number of repetitions

Strength: the ability to exert force against resistance

Variable resistance training: the use of a machine that adjusts the resistance through the range of movement of a muscle contraction to accommodate to the change in muscle strength at different joint angles

Weight lifting: competition that requires the participants to use specific lifts

Weight training: a systematic series of resistance exercises to develop strength

STRENGTH PROGRAMS

Strength development programs are basically either *dynamic* (muscle actions with movement) or *isometric* (muscle actions with little or no movement).

The most common type of training program is one using dynamic actions. The major advantage of this system is that it brings about strength gains through a full range of motion. As a muscle goes through a range of motion, it must receive adequate resistance at all of the joint angles to stimulate strength increases. For example, if resistance is incurred at only the 90° angle, this is where the muscle will be stronger, not at the other angles, where resistance is not encountered. Dynamic training seems to have a greater effect on muscle hypertrophy, muscle endurance, increased flexibility, and development of connective tissue. This type of training also allows the individual to observe the work being done, which can be a source of satisfaction from a psychological standpoint.

From a cosmetic viewpoint, the gains made from a dynamic program are greater than those from an isometric program. Since many people engage in strength programs for body changes related to training, this is an added benefit for dynamic training.

Some advantages ascribed to an isometric training program are that it requires less equipment and usually causes little muscle soreness. This mode of training makes it possible to isolate specific joint angles to strengthen. In one program, specific isometric actions with the leg muscles were used to increase the ability of various athletes to jump higher and farther. The primary training program, however, for the athletes was dynamic; isometric exercises were utilized to supplement this program.

A disadvantage of isometric training is that it may causes high systolic and diastolic blood pressures, which might be harmful to the heart and circulatory system.

MACHINES VS. FREE WEIGHTS

In the past few years, as interest in the development of strength has increased, a dazzling array of exercise machines has appeared on the market. Advertisements use highly persuasive language to explain why their specific machines are best and why all other machines and training methods will soon be obsolete. Many advertisements contain testimonies from prominent athletes or coaches.

With the development of these machines have come new terms in strength training: *isokinetic* and *variable resistance*. As a muscle goes through a range of motion, the ability of the lever system to exert force changes at different angles. Thus the amount of weight that can be lifted is limited by the weakest point in the range of motion. Therefore many manufacturers of equipment have developed machines that theoretically have the ability to adjust the resistance of the machine to the muscle's ability to exert force. The claim is that these machines will bring about a faster and greater increase of strength through the full range of motion.

The other type of training devices are sometimes referred to as *free weights*. Free weights include barbells, dumbbells, and other related equipment. In the early 1900s, Allan Calvert developed adjustable barbells, with which weighted plates could be added or taken off to change the resistance. In over one hundred years, few changes have been made to alter his basic design.

Many discussions have taken place regarding the merits of machines versus free weights. Some observers believe that it is not an either-or problem; rather, a trainer should use many different methods in strength training. As long as the basic principles regarding strength development are observed, making strength gains and body changes with both machines and free weights are possible. Being consistent in your training in the program you choose is probably more important than the type of training device you select. The best recommendation is to experiment with different exercises and various types of training equipment and use them to develop a personalized program.

NUTRITION AND STRENGTH DEVELOPMENT

Nutrition affects virtually every function of the body. Nutrients from food are necessary for every heartbeat, nerve sensation, and muscle contraction.

Nutrients are chemical substances obtained from food during digestion. About fifty nutrients, including water, are needed daily for optimum health. No single substance will maintain good health. Although specific nutrients are known to have important functions in specific parts of the body, even those nutrients are dependent upon the presence of other nutrients for their best effects. An effort should be made to attain and maintain an adequate, balanced daily intake of all the necessary nutrients throughout life.

FOOD PYRAMID

In 2005, the U.S. Department of Agriculture (USDA) released a new food pyramid (My Pyramid). Unlike previous food pyramids, which were one-size-fits-all dietary recommendations, My Pyramid is designed to meet the needs of an individual based on age, gender, and activity level.

My Pyramid incorporates recommendations from the 2005 Dietary Guidelines for Americans, which was released by the U.S. Department of Health and Human Services (HHS) in January 2005. The Dietary Guidelines for Americans provide authoritative advice for people two years of age and older about how proper dietary habits can promote health and reduce the risk of major chronic diseases.

Figure 2.9 is an example of the My Pyramid.

The My Pyramid contains a variety of helpful messages. Following are examples of the messages compiled by the USDA.

- Personalization, demonstration by the MyPyramid Web site. To find a personalized recommendation of the kinds and amounts of food to eat each day, go to MyPyramid.gov.
- Gradual improvement, encouraged by the slogan, "Steps to a Healthier You." It suggests that individuals can benefit from taking small steps to improve their diet and lifestyle each day.
- Physical activity, represented by the steps and the person climbing them, as a reminder of the importance of daily physical activity.
- Variety, symbolized by the six color bands representing the five food groups of MyPyramid and oils. Foods from all groups are needed each day for good health.
- Moderation, represented by the narrowing of each food group from bottom to top. The wider base stands for foods with little or no solid fats, added sugars, or caloric sweeteners. These should be selected more often to get the most nutrition from calories consumed.
- Proportionality, shown by the different widths of the food group bands. The widths suggest how much food a person should choose from each group. The widths are just a general guide, not exact proportions. Check MyPyramid.gov for the amount that is right for you.

The new food guidance system utilizes interactive technology found on MyPyramid.gov. MyPyramid contains interactive activities that make it easy for individuals to key in their age, gender and physical activity level so that they can get a more personalized recommendation on their daily calorie level based on the *2005 Dietary Guidelines for Americans*. It also allows individuals to find general food guidance and suggestions for making smart choices from each food group.

MyPyramid.gov Features

- MyPyramid Plan—provides a quick estimate of what and how much food you should eat from the different food groups by entering your age, gender and activity level.
- MyPyramid Tracker—provides more detailed information on your diet quality and physical activity status by comparing a day's worth of foods eaten with current nutrition guidance. Relevant nutrition and physical activity messages are tailored to your desire to maintain your current weight or to lose weight.
- Inside MyPyramid—provides in-depth information for every food group, including recommended daily amounts in commonly used measures, like cups and ounces, with examples and everyday tips. The section also includes recommendations for choosing healthy oils, discretionary calories and physical activity.

Anatomy of MyPyramid

One size doesn't fit all
USDA's new MyPyramid symbolizes a personalized approach to healthy eating and physical activity. The symbol has been designed to be simple. It has been developed to remind consumers to make healthy food choices and to be active every day. The different parts of the symbol are described below.

Proportionality
Proportionality is shown by the different widths of the food group bands. The widths suggest how much food a person should choose from each group. The widths are just a general guide, not exact proportions. Check the Web site for how much is right for you.

Variety
Variety is symbolized by the 6 color bands representing the 5 food groups of the Pyramid and oils. This illustrates that foods from all groups are needed each day for good health.

Gradual Improvement
Gradual improvement is encouraged by the slogan. It suggests that individuals can benefit from taking small steps to improve their diet and lifestyle each day.

Activity
Activity is represented by the steps and the person climbing them, as a reminder of the important of daily physical activity.

Moderation
Moderation is presented by the narrowing of each food group from bottom to top. The wider base stands for foods with little or no solid fats or added sugars. These should be selected more often. The narrower top area stands for foods containing more added sugars and solid fats. The more active you are, the more of these foods can fit into your diet.

Personalization
Personalization is shown by the person on the steps, the slogan, and the URL. Find the kinds and amounts of food to eat each day at MyPyramid.gov.

MyPyramid.gov
STEPS TO A HEALTHIER YOU

| GRAINS | VEGETABLES | FRUITS | OILS | MILK | MEATS & BEANS |

Figure 2.9

USDA US Department of Agriculture
Center for Nutrition Policy
and Promotion
April 2005 CNPP-16

USDA is an equal opportunity provider and employer.

- Start Today—provides tips and resources that include downloadable suggestions on all the food groups and physical activity, and a worksheet to track what you are eating.

Future enhancements to MyPyramid.gov will include features that make it possible for consumers to make specific food choices by group, look at everyday portions of favorite foods and adjust their choices to meet their daily needs.

A child-friendly version of MyPyramid for teachers and children has also been developed. This version of MyPyramid is intended to reach children 6 to 11 years old with targeted messages about the importance of making smart eating and physical activity choices. Additional information about USDA's MyPyramid is available at MyPyramid.gov. The *2005 Dietary Guidelines for Americans* and consumer brochure are available at www.healthierus.gov/dietaryguidelines

The My Pyramid guide has the advantages of simplicity and enough freedom of choice to fit individual choices and different economic levels.

Many times a person starting a strength training program becomes concerned about a need for extra protein in the diet. Hoping to increase body size and strength, many individuals have been attracted to high-protein diets and concentrated protein supplements. There is no scientific evidence that supports the belief that people engaging in strength programs require increased amounts of protein. The National Research Council recommends that both men and women consume one to two grams of protein per kilogram (2.2 lbs.) of body weight. The average American ingests two or three times as much protein as needed. Uncontrolled protein intake in the diet has some drawbacks. High-protein diets are dehydrating because they demand large amounts of water for urinary excretion of the metabolic by-products. Protein supplements may cause loss of appetite and diarrhea, and excess protein may also be changed to fat, stored in the body, and contribute to obesity.

The MyPyramid plan provides abundant protein and is the best nutritional program to follow for a training program.

A factor that may influence the use of protein in the production of muscle tissue is the timing of protein intake. There appears to be a "window of opportunity" when both protein and carbohydrate will be assimilated into the body at a faster rate. This time frame seems to be immediately after a strenuous strength work-out and then begins to diminish in the next two hours.

A product that is relatively cheap and might affect protein synthesis is chocolate milk. One pint of chocolate milk contains 260 calories, 16 grams of complete protein (this means it contains all of the essential amino acids that can't be produced by the body), 48 grams of carbohydrate, 4 grams of fat, and 600 milligrams of calcium. Chocolate milk is preferred over white milk since the high glycemic index of the carbohydrate may increase the absorption of the protein and carbohydrate.

Milk contains two unique kinds of protein, known as whey protein and casein protein. Whey protein is absorbed quite rapidly and the casein protein is taken up more slowly. By using milk, the body now has a product that will provide the muscle cells with an intake of amino acids for an extended period of time.

It should be noted that milk contains lactose and one should be aware if they are unable to tolerate lactose.

It is also important to remember that it is the combining of a strength work-out with the ingestion of nutrients that is important. The strength work-out is the trigger that brings about the chemical changes that affects the increase in lean body mass that contributes to increased strength.

DIETARY SUPPLEMENTS

The dietary supplement industry is a multi-billion dollar business in the United States. Caution is needed in the use of these products as, unlike medications, dietary supplements do not have to be approved by the Food and Drug Administration (FDA) in regards to either safety or effectiveness. Some dietary supplements may even contain banned substances such as androstenedrone and ephedrine. Something may appear to be harmless, but when used in combination with other substances may cause a person to fail a drug test.

Ellen Coleman, a registered dietitian and a nutrition consultant for the Los Angeles Lakers and the Anaheim Angels, gives excellent advice when considering any dietary supplement.

1. Carry USP (United States Pharmacopeia) on the label. USP means that the supplement passes tests for dissolution (how well it dissolves); disintegration (loss or separation of the component parts of a substance); potency, and purity. The manufacturer should be able to demonstrate that the product passes tests for content potency, purity, and uniformity.
2. Made by nationally known food and drug manufacturers. Reputable manufacturers follow strict quality control procedures. If the company does not answer questions or address complaints, do not use their product.
3. Supported by research. Reputable companies should provide research from peer-reviewed journals to support claims. Endorsements from well-known athletes or individuals are not an example of peer-reviewed research.
4. Accurate and appropriate claims. If statements are unclear or the label makes preposterous claims, it is unlikely the company follows good quality control procedures. If the claims sound too good to be true, be wary.
5. Talk with a doctor or pharmacist about dietary supplements. Some products may interact with prescription and over-the-counter medications as well as other supplements and cause potentially serious adverse effects.

Table 2.2 contains a list of dietary supplements that propose to increase athletic ability. This table gives the name of the supplement, the claimed benefits, and also the efficacy and safety concerns to be considered when using these products.

ANABOLIC STEROIDS

Over the years individuals have taken anabolic steroids in an attempt to obtain increased muscle mass and strength. Steroids are artificial male hormones that have anabolic properties; that is, they cause a buildup of complex chemical units, such as muscle protein. There is much contradictory research as to whether the steroids accomplish their intended purpose. Anabolic steroids are banned by every international sports federation, and in some cases athletes have been banned from competition for using these drugs. The position statement that follows, from the American College of Sports Medicine, details some of the problems associated with their use. A person using anabolic steroids should consult first with a medical doctor and use them only under the doctor's supervision.

Based on a comprehensive survey of the world literature and a careful analysis of the claims made for and against the efficacy of anabolic-androgenic steroids in improving human physical performance, the position of the American College of Sports Medicine is as follows:

1. The administration of anabolic-androgenic steroids to healthy humans below age fifty in medically approved therapeutic doses often does not of itself bring about any significant improvements in strength, aerobic endurance, lean body mass, or body weight.

Table 2.2   Dietary Supplements Used by Athletes

Dietary Supplement	Claimed Benefits
Amino acids—branched chain *Leucine, isoleucine, valine*	■ Increases endurance ■ Postpones onset of fatigue ■ Increases weight/strength ■ Prevents muscle breakdown
Amino acids—individual *Building blocks of protein*	Arginine and ornithine ■ Growth hormone releasers ■ Decreases body fat ■ Increases weight/muscle Tryptophan ■ Relieves insomnia, depression, and PMS ■ Increases growth hormone ■ Enhances performance
Amino acids—mixtures *Partially digested proteins*	■ Increases muscle mass ■ Faster protein absorption
Aspartates *Organic salt*	■ Increases energy ■ Enhances fat metabolism ■ Spares glycogen ■ Postpones fatigue
Bicarbonates *Buffer*	■ Facilitates performance in high-power events ■ Decreases acid buildup that limits carbohydrate metabolism and induces fatigue
Boron *Nonessential trace mineral*	■ Natural testosterone booster ■ Increases weight/muscle
Caffeine *Central nervous system stimulant found in coffee, tea, chocolate, soft drinks, and over-the-counter drugs*	■ Increases endurance performance ■ Increases fat oxidation ■ Increases motivation and postpones fatigue ■ Increases short-term, intense exercise performance
Carnitine *Vitamin-like molecule synthesized from glutamate and methionine*	■ Increases fatty acid oxidation (carbohydrate sparing) ■ Fat loss (cutting) agent

Efficacy	Safety/Other Concerns
■ Appear to be metabolized at a higher rate during endurance exercise ■ Research on the effects of supplementation on endurance performance is still elusive	■ Safety thresholds of individual amino acids are not known
■ Effects of arginine and ornithine remain to be proven; more research is warranted ■ Tryptophan may have ergogenic benefits, but performance detriments (drowsiness, impaired glucose metabolism) and safety concerns have been shown ■ Few performance-enhancing effects of individual amino acids have been proven	■ Safety threshold of individual amino acids is not known; can pose serious risks to certain people: pregnant or nursing women, infants, children, adolescents, older adults, individuals with disorders in protein metabolism ■ Tryptophan banned by FDA in 1990 due to reports of eosinophilia myalgia syndrome and resulting deaths
■ No benefits for healthy adults with adequate protein intake ■ Little evidence to support muscle gains	■ Safety is questionable
■ Research on benefits is inconclusive	■ Small doses appear to pose minimal risk
■ Conflicting evidence	■ Can produce GI distress ■ Banned by governing bodies of some sports
■ A study on postmenopausal women showed increased testosterone levels with boron supplementation; effects on weight and muscle were not evaluated ■ Inconclusive evidence	■ Safety data not located
■ Use of 3–6 mg/kg body weight can produce endurance benefits without adverse side effects or reaching illegal limits for sports competition ■ Effects on short-term, intense exercise have not been well examined	■ Can cause anxiety, jitters, GI discomfort, insomnia, irritability, and arrhythmias ■ Wide variation of responses ■ Diuretic effect of caffeine can promote dehydration ■ Considered a "controlled or restricted substance" by IOC
■ Benefits not substantiated ■ No scientific basis to promote use by athletes	■ Appears to be safe ■ Large doses can cause diarrhea

Continued.

Table 2.2   Dietary Supplements Used by Athletes–Continued

Dietary Supplement	Claimed Benefits
Ciwujia *Chinese herb derived from root*	■ Traditional Chinese medicine used to treat fatigue and boost immune function; used for 1,700 years ■ Increases fat metabolism; spares glycogen ■ Decreases lactic acid buildup ■ Decreases heart rate
Choline *Precursor of neurotransmitter, acetylcholine; found in lecithin*	■ Fat loss (cutting) agent ■ Enhances endurance performance
Chromium compounds (chromium piccolinate) *Essential trace mineral*	■ Increases weight/muscle ■ Insulin enhancer ■ Increases glycogen stores ■ Regulates fat deposition and decreases body fat
Coenzyme Q10 (CoQ10) *Type of fat found in mitochondria*	■ Increase oxygen uptake ■ Increase exercise performance
Creatine *Substance involved in energy metabolism; cellular component*	■ Promotes phosphocreatine and ATP resynthesis during anaerobic work ■ Enhances anaerobic performance ■ Allows athlete to train longer at higher intensities without fatigue
Dibencozide *Cobalt-containing organic compound*	■ Increases weight/muscle ■ Active form of vitamin B12 ■ Steroid alternative
Dessicated liver *Powder made from animal liver*	■ Good source of protein, iron, zinc, and B vitamins ■ Increases energy and endurance
Ferulic acid (ȳ-oryzanol) *Plant sterol*	■ Increases weight/muscle ■ Increases testosterone and growth hormone secretions ■ Antioxidant ■ Increases endorphins

Efficacy	Safety/Other Concerns

■ Chinese studies done on animals
■ American studies have several design flaws:
  ■ small number of subjects
  ■ not double blind
  ■ lack of controls
  ■ subjects weren't athletes
  ■ exercise was only of moderate intensity
  ■ exercise ≤60 minutes
	■ Manufacturer claims substance is remarkably safe
	■ No other safety data located

■ Effects on fat loss are largely theoretical ■ Possible benefits in latter stages of endurance performance (greater than 15 miles), but more research is needed	■ Nontoxic ■ Large doses cause diarrhea ■ Large doses emit a fishy smell
■ Endurance exercise increases urinary losses of chromium ■ Studies showing increases in muscle mass were poorly controlled ■ Anabolic effects are inconclusive	■ Estimated safe and adequate daily dietary intake is 50–200 micrograms/day ■ Minimal risk of toxicity from oral supplementation
■ Therapeutic use in cardiac patients shows promise ■ Research on healthy athletes does not show same effects	■ Safety data not located

■ Shows promise
■ More research needed to:
  ■ substantiate benefits
  ■ elucidate mechanisms
  ■ establish safe/effective dosages
■ Vegetarian athletes have lower creatine pool and are likely to benefit
	■ Ingestion of 20 mg/day for 5 days appears to present minimal risk
	■ Excesses excreted by kidneys

■ No substantiation for anabolic benefits ■ Cobalamin is the active form of B12	■ Safety data not located
■ Effects small in context of total diet	■ Safety data not located
■ Based on anecdotal evidence ■ No controlled research to support anabolic claims ■ Metabolized in GI tract, poorly absorbed, does not enter bloodstream intact ■ Endorphin effect may have some basis, but more research is needed	■ Low toxicity ■ Individuals with lipid storage disease may get xanthomatosis (nodular yellowish fat deposits around eyelids and on hands)

Continued.

Table 2.2   Dietary Supplements Used by Athletes—Continued

Dietary Supplement	Claimed Benefits
Ginseng *Extract of ginseng root*	■ Protects against tissue damage ■ Decreases lactate buildup ■ Increases VO_{2max}
Inosine *Nucleoside, substance involved in energy metabolism*	■ Activates cellular function ■ Enhances endurance ■ Stimulates ATP production; aids exercise intensity ■ Promotes strength
Ma huang (squaw tea, Mormon tea, ephedra) *Herbal supplement*	■ Controls weight ■ Boosts energy
Medium chain triglycerides (MTC) *Short fat molecules which are more readily absorbed*	■ Increases energy ■ Decreases body fat ■ Increases muscle ■ Enhances metabolism and extends endurance ■ Decreases serum cholesterol
Pangamic acid (calcium pangamate, vitamin B15) *Organic chemical*	■ Increase muscle glycogen ■ Enhance aerobic metabolism ■ Vitamin essential to health
Phosphate salts *Buffer*	■ Facilitates performance in high-power events ■ Decreases acid buildup that limits carbohydrate metabolism and induces fatigue ■ Stimulates carbohydrate metabolism and enhances anaerobic performance
Sarsparilla (Smilax) *Plant sterol*	■ Increases weight/muscle ■ Natural form of testosterone
Yohimbe (yohimbine) *Tree bark containing druglike chemicals*	■ Aphrodisiac ■ Treatment for impotence ■ Natural testosterone

Source: Adapted from Jean Starlie, "A Strategy for Supplements," Training and Conditioning 7, no. 4 (August 1997). Reprinted with permission of publisher.

Note: The literature reviewed to compile this table did not discuss the safety of numerous supplements. Other sources were consulted, but in several cases data could not be located.

Efficacy	Safety/Other Concerns
■ Conflicting evidence	■ High doses cause elevated blood pressure, nervousness, and confusion
■ Minimal supporting evidence from rat studies; human studies refute claim ■ Some studies show impaired performance ■ Does not appear to be an effective ergogenic aid	■ Uric acid is by-product, so individuals with predisposition to gout and kidney stones should avoid inosine
	■ Numerous reports of adverse effects: liver failure, elevated blood pressure, palpitations, strokes ■ 20 documented deaths ■ When combined with caffeine, raises potential for harmful effects ■ IOC bans use of ephedra
■ Effective for people with malabsorption disorders ■ Effectiveness in athletes not documented	■ Not safe for people with liver disease and diabetes
■ Claims based on animal studies from Soviet Union ■ Several well-controlled studies in U.S. have showed no effect on cardiovascular and metabolic responses to exercise ■ No essentiality to human nutrition established	■ FDA-approved additive with no margin of safety
■ Inconclusive evidence	■ Low doses appear to pose minimal risk ■ Some people experience gastrointestinal distress
■ Based on practices of early Central American Indians ■ No supporting research	■ Safety data not located
■ Effectiveness unknown and questionable	■ Serious adverse effects reported: kidney failure, seizures, and death ■ Side effects include anxiety attacks, elevated blood pressure ■ Serious adverse interactions when taken with liver, cheese, red wine and some over-the-counter-drugs (e.g., decongestants)

2. There is no conclusive scientific evidence that extremely large doses of anabolic-androgenic steroids either aid or hinder athletic performance.
3. The prolonged use of oral anabolic-androgenic steroids (C_{17}-alkylated derivatives of testosterone) has resulted in liver disorders in some persons. Some of these disorders are apparently reversible with the cessation of drug usage, but others are not.
4. The administration of anabolic-androgenic steroids to male humans may result in a decrease in testicular size and function and a decrease in sperm production. Although these effects appear to be reversible when small doses of steroids are used for short periods of time, the reversibility of the effects of large doses over extended periods of time is unclear.
5. Serious and continuing efforts should be made to educate male and female athletes, coaches, physical educators, physicians, trainers, and the general public regarding the inconsistent effects of anabolic-androgenic steroids on improvement of human physical performance and the potential dangers of taking certain forms of these substances, especially in large doses, for prolonged periods.

GAINING BODY WEIGHT

Dr. Melvin Williams, the director of the Human Performance Laboratory at Old Dominion University, has developed excellent guidelines to help maximize gains in muscle tissue and keep body fat increases relatively low:

1. Set a reasonable goal within a certain time period. The greatest gains will be made in the first three months; in untrained young men, this can be approximately three pounds per month. In well-trained athletes and women, the gains will be much less. Gender and genetics are two of the major controlling factors in how much and how fast the lean body mass will be gained. After a few years of dietary intervention and training, the gains are reduced and may be limited to about 1 to 3 percent per year.
2. Increase your caloric intake. To add a pound of muscle tissue per week, you need to increase your caloric intake by approximately four hundred calories, and you need about fourteen grams of additional protein per day. One glass of skim milk, three slices of whole wheat bread, and two hard-boiled egg whites will provide the necessary calories and about twenty-three grams of protein.

   Many people assume that protein is the important food for increasing muscle mass, but total energy intake, primarily from carbohydrates, is what allows the body to train and to bring about the increased gain in muscle size. A more specific guideline for the total amount of protein needed is that an intake of one to two grams of protein per day for each 2.2 pounds of body weight will adequately meet the needs of a weight gain program.
3. Start a strength training exercise program. It is not the intake of food that provides the stimulus for increased muscle mass; rather, the use of the overload principle in a strength training program is what causes the muscles to increase in size.
4. Use a tape measure to take body measurements. Be sure to take them at the same place every one to two weeks. Body parts measured should include the neck, upper and lower arm, chest, abdomen, thigh, and calf. This measuring is to ensure that body weight gains are proportionately distributed. You should look for good gains in the chest and limbs, but the abdominal girth increase should be kept low because that is where fat usually increases the most. Appendix A contains a body measurement chart to record your measurements.
5. Beware of misleading information concerning dietary supplements that promise to effectively increase the amount of lean muscle mass. Many people who go on a weight gaining and strength training program have questions about the use of nutrition supplements. Table 2.2 contains information that will give you valid answers concerning the use of many of these so-called nutritional aids. As indicated, most advertised claims are speculative, since very little well-controlled research has been conducted for most of these purported nutritional supplements.

   By following these suggestions, you can plan a program that will be very effective in gaining the proper kind of body weight.

3

Variables in a Strength Training Program

A well-designed program to develop strength and reduce the chance of injury must take into consideration the following variables:

1. Resistance to utilize
2. Number of repetitions
3. Number of sets
4. Rest interval between sets
5. Frequency of workouts during the week
6. Safety procedures

A systematic overloading of a muscle increases the strength and size of the muscle. Four possible methods can be used to increase the difficulty of a strength workout:

1. Increase the resistance
2. Increase the repetitions
3. Increase the number of sets
4. Decrease the time of the rest intervals between sets

▌ **RESISTANCE**

The greatest strength gains seem to be obtained when the resistance is increased and the other variables are held constant. The *minimum* resistance that can be used and still get strength gains is approximately 60 percent of the maximum force or weight lifted for one muscle contraction. The maximum force that can be exerted is referred to as the 1 RM.

It might appear that the fastest way to obtain strength would be to do exercises that require a single repetition of maximum force. However, the problem with this type of training is that it may cause injury to the muscle or connective tissue. It may also lead to chronic fatigue of the muscle and retard the progress toward increased strength and muscle development.

Since it is difficult to determine exactly how much weight a person should be lifting for each exercise, some guidelines are needed. Through the years the "guesstimate" method of determining resistance has been utilized with great success. This method has been used with both beginning weight training classes and elite athletes. The process is one of trial and error.

1. Guess how many pounds you can lift for a specific exercise.
2. Try this weight for the given number of repetitions for one set, i.e., 6 RM, 10 RM, and so on.
3. If the exercise is too easy and you can do more than the recommended number of repetitions, increase the resistance for the next set.
4. If the exercise is too hard and you cannot do the recommended number of repetitions, decrease the resistance for the next set.
5. Remember to increase the weight for the next workout whenever you can do more than the recommended number of repetitions on the last set of an exercise.

REPETITIONS

Resistance exceeding 60 percent of maximum has been found to be very effective in bringing about strength gains in a training program. When you use between 5 and 12 RM, over 70 percent of the repetitions will be above 60 percent of the 1 RM and will thus ensure that you are obtaining a proper training stimulus. A rule of thumb that works well in determining the weight load to use in an exercise is as follows:

If your objective is increased muscle strength then decrease the repetitions, increase the resistance.

If your objective is increased muscle endurance then increase the repetitions, decrease the resistance.

Thus an athlete wishes a greater increase in strength might use 5 RM, and an athlete who needs muscle endurance might use 15 RM.

SETS

The most popular and versatile system of strength development is the set system, in which an individual performs an exercise for a given number of repetitions, rests for an interval of time, and repeats the exercise for a given number of sets. This system can be adapted to any objective in strength development for the beginner, the bodybuilder, the athlete, or the advanced weight lifter.

Most beginning weight trainers make good progress by using a program consisting of three or four sets using 6 to 10 RM in each set.

One Set Only

The excuse that many people use for not exercising is that they don't have enough time. For instance, ten different exercises for three sets and ten repetitions with a two-minute recovery between each set would take approximately ninety minutes. If you did only one set of ten different exercises and went from one body part to the next without a recovery, then the workout time could be reduced to less than twenty minutes—certainly a reasonable amount of time to be allotted to strength training. Research studies have shown that one set of 6 to 10 RM is effective for providing a strength stimulus that will produce significant strength gains.

People who train on Nautilus machines are recommended to do only one set of 8 to 12 RM. Olympic weight lifters and power lifters often train using five to ten sets of 1 to 5 RM each set. Bodybuilders may utilize five to ten sets of 10 to 15 RM in their workouts.

Volume

If a major goal is to increase muscle mass, the volume of the workout (sets and repetitions) may need to be increased. There is a relationship between increased hypertrophy and increased volume. The following are some of the reasons that are thought to influence this relationship:

1. Increased volume may stimulate the activation of a maximum number of muscle cells and increase the tension being placed on the contractile fibrils.
2. Increased volume may cause an increase in the secretion of anabolic hormones, which are some of the chemical modulators that stimulate the growth of muscle tissue.
3. Increased volume may cause muscle cells to use an energy-releasing system (anaerobic glycolysis) that produces lactic acid. An accumulation of lactic acid may promote an increase in the production of anabolic hormones such as testosterone and human growth hormone. These anabolic hormones in turn stimulate protein synthesis in the muscle cell and an increase in contractile filaments with an increase in muscle cell size.
4. Increased volume may augment myofibrilar hydration, or the "muscle pump," which may stimulate protein synthesis and inhibit protein breakdown in the muscle cell.

To obtain a "muscle pump" the attempt is to force more fluid into the muscle cells being exercised. This can be accomplished by increasing the number of repetitions per set and by increasing the number of exercises for a given muscle group.

If your goal is to increase muscle mass, then you might do multiple exercises with three to five sets of eight to twelve repetitions with a two-minute recovery between sets. For example, you might do three different exercises for the biceps of the arm using four sets per exercise and ten repetitions per set. The chapter on bodybuilding provides examples of various training routines that might be utilized to manipulate the volume to obtain increased muscle hypertrophy.

Each exercise should commence with a warm-up set of a lighter weight. A set of ten repetitions using 50 percent of the maximum weight that can be lifted works very well as a warm-up set. This will help to reduce injury and prepare the muscle system for additional resistance in the following sets.

REST INTERVAL BETWEEN SETS

The rest interval between sets is an important consideration in designing a strength training program. The amount of time taken between sets is determined by individual training objectives. For example, bodybuilders usually take very short rest periods, while weight lifters and athletes training with near to maximum weight loads require relatively extended rest periods between sets.

One way to determine the rest interval is to be aware of the primary energy sources required in the lifting of weights. This energy source, which is composed of the chemicals adenosine triphosphate and phosphocreatine, is known as the *phosphagen stores*. These phosphagen stores have the ability to provide maximum energy for short periods of time and usually last for no more than ten seconds.

Table 3.1	Replenishment of Phosphagen Stores

Rest Time	Approximate Percentage of Phosphagen Stores Replenished
0 seconds	0.00
30 seconds	50.00
60 seconds (1 minute)	75.00
90 seconds	87.50
120 seconds (2 minutes)	93.75
150 seconds	96.88
180 seconds (3 minutes)	98.44
210 seconds	99.22
240 seconds (4 minutes)	99.61
270 seconds	99.80
300 seconds (5 minutes)	99.90

These stores are quickly replenished in the rest interval. Within thirty seconds, approximately 50 percent of the phosphagens are resynthesized and available for another bout of exercise. Table 3.1 shows the amount of rest time and the approximate percentage of phosphagen stores replenished.

As indicated by Table 3.1, most of the phosphagen stores are replenished within two minutes. Individuals, such as bodybuilders, who wish to obtain the so-called muscle pump, might use one-minute intervals. Those who are lifting near-maximum weight would increase the rest interval to three or more minutes. In most cases, a rest interval of approximately two minutes should be an adequate amount of time.

The recovery is specific to the muscles involved in the exercise. To reduce the time necessary to complete a workout, one could alternate sets of different exercises. For example, do a set using the chest muscles, such as the bench press, and a set utilizing the legs, such as the leg press. Do the exercises until the required number of sets is completed, and then you can move on to two different exercises.

WORKOUT FREQUENCY

When the body systems, such as the muscular system, are overloaded, cells require a certain amount of time to recover and undergo the physiological changes that are involved in training. If the recovery time is too short, the muscle cells are unable to accommodate and rebuild to ensure a higher level of strength. This can lead to chronic fatigue and may even result in a loss of strength. A decrease in performance is the best indicator that a person needs more rest and a decrease in work.

Most strength workouts require a rest day between each workout day for the various muscle groups exercised. A muscle group should be trained on three nonconsecutive days each week, such as Monday, Wednesday, and Friday. In chapter 7, Bodybuilding and Physique Training, a type of training known as the split-body routine is explained. Using this routine, a person can work out every day by exercising one part of the body one day, then letting it rest while training another body part on the next day.

A person can train any time during the day. Training time is usually determined by the amount of time available and when training facilities can be used.

AMERICAN COLLEGE OF SPORTS MEDICINE GUIDELINES

The American College of Sports Medicine makes the following recommendations, which apply to exercises for individuals at all levels. These suggestions will be helpful in obtaining good results with strength training.

1. Strength training exercises should involve both eccentric and concentric actions.
2. Exercises should involve single joints and multiple joints for beginners, intermediates, and advanced lifters. When maximum power output is the goal, a majority of the exercises should involve mostly multiple-joint lifts.
3. Exercise large muscle groups before small muscle groups, multiple-joint exercises before single-joint exercises, and high-intensity exercises before those of lower intensity.
4. Generally, the order of exercises should be from large to small, from multiple-joint exercise to single-joint, from high intensity to low intensity, and from most complex to least complex.
5. Periodization, which is explained in chapter 6, allows the strength trainer to use variety in sequencing exercises.

SAFETY PROCEDURES

An examination of the accidents in various activities reveals that weight training is one of the safest forms of recreation a person can participate in. However, some common sense rules should be followed.

If a person has been sedentary for a long period and suspects some medical problem, a good physical examination by a qualified physician would be wise.

Frederick C. Hatfield and March L. Krotee, in their book *Personalized Weight Training for Fitness and Athletics: From Theory to Practice,* have compiled a list of recommended guidelines that is excellent advice for any weight trainer:

1. Never train alone. Injuries and accidents can often be avoided when someone else is present. It's also more fun to involve others as either a primary or secondary partner. A weight training room should be supervised by trained personnel.
2. Inspect equipment, read instructions, and have a qualified instructor demonstrate each piece of equipment. In short, if you don't know what you're doing, seek professional advice and guidance. Your chances of reaching your training aims and objectives will be greatly enhanced.
3. Use experienced spotters whenever necessary. Heavy squats and bench presses are especially dangerous, and under no circumstances should they be attempted without one or two knowledgeable spotters. Other exercises such as good mornings, hyperextensions, and incline or decline presses also require spotting.

4. Keep alert and lift weights or engage in associated physical activity in designated areas only. With multiuse equipment, be aware of where you are as well as the location of others around you. Be careful not to walk directly in front of lifters, as you may startle them, disturb their concentration, or even inadvertently bump into their equipment.

5. Always check your weights and immediate training environment before each set. Be sure that even loading is followed, collars are tightened, and barbell sleeves are free to revolve. Count your weight!

6. Use equipment as it was designed to be employed. Improper use can cause injury, equipment breakdowns, and lost training time.

7. Keep lifting and exercise areas clean, neat, and orderly. Place weights in designated areas after using, as misplaced weights are often the cause of injury.

8. When using weight training machines, carefully check all cables, pulleys, selector keys (use appropriate key, not a substitute), nuts, bolts, cam chains, seat adjustments, and belts for maximum safety. The equipment should also be kept clean and appropriately lubricated. If equipment jams, do not attempt to free it yourself. Report all problems immediately to the weight training supervisor.

9. Wear proper lifting attire and remember that perspiration causes slippery equipment and skin—both dangerous conditions. Don't lift in your stocking feet.

10. Use proper breathing techniques when lifting. If a person takes a deep breath and holds it while straining to lift the weight, this can significantly decrease the blood flow to an area of the body. The increased pressure in the chest cavity that can result when holding the breath can hinder the venous blood return to the heart and elevate blood pressure. This is known as the *Valsalva effect.*

    To assure that you have proper breathing procedures in strength training:
    a. Remove the bar from the rack or apply pressure to the resistance lever if using a machine and stabilize the weight.
    b. Inspire deeply, thus stabilizing the appropriate body structures.
    c. Lower the weight (eccentric action).
    d. Raise the weight (concentric action) and expire during the last one-half to two-thirds of the upward movement.
    e. Repeat the cycle.
    f. Always keep the mouth open.

11. Don't lift if an injury may be aggravated. Temporarily modify the activity to exclude the injured area or associated muscle group.

12. If you're not feeling well or even up to par, you should temporarily suspend lifting. When recovering from an illness, resume lifting at a level of intensity and weight level well below that achieved before the illness.

13. Attend to weight training through a planned personalized program of progressive resistance training. This will reduce muscle soreness and aching joints and tendons, and will reduce your chance for injury. Proper technique and supervision in a professionally developed weight training program are mandatory.

14. Be aware of environmental conditions such as room temperature, humidity, altitude, and pollution count, and adapt your weight lifting program accordingly.

15. Don't lift immediately after a heavy meal.

16. Excessively hot showers should be avoided immediately after training. In some rare instances, hot showers have been associated with manifestations of myocardial infarction or heart attack.

17. Weight training does not have to be highly competitive in nature to be healthful. In fact, spontaneous and unwarranted 1 RMs, such as trying to outlift a colleague, often leads to a loss of safety focus concerning the physiological boundaries for safe participation.

18. As part of the physiological and psychological preparation for weight training, the warm-up may be considered a safety precaution. Warm-up is a preparation that is conducted at submaximal effort for a duration of approximately five to fifteen minutes immediately before engaging in lifting. Warm-up should be intense enough to increase body temperature and cause perspiration, but should not require a longer duration of submaximal effort. The value of warm-up seems to be quite controversial for participation in various sport spe-

cific situations; however, for the individual engaging in regular, vigorous weight training, warm-up is deemed a vital safety factor.

WEIGHT LIFTING BELTS

Weight lifting belts have been used for many years. The purpose of the belt is to add support to the lumbar spine and lower back during heavy lifts. Research indicates that using a belt may bring about an increase in intra-abdominal pressure. This increase in pressure allows all of the contents within the abdominal cavity to share compression loads that might otherwise have a negative effect on the spine.

If the goal is to lift the maximum amount of weight possible or to do a given exercise to complete fatigue, then the use of a weight lifting belt might be beneficial. Using a belt might bring about a 5 to 15 percent increase in the amount of weight lifted in such exercises as the squat, dead lift, and power clean. Some research indicates that weight lifting belts may delay the onset of fatigue when doing many repetitions in the squat by adding support to the body.

Using weight lifting belts can have disadvantages as well. Doing maximum lifts or lifting to exhaustion might increase the probability of injury. Training to failure is not necessary for strength development. When you use a weight lifting belt, supporting muscles that can cause increased intra-abdominal pressure might do the opposite of what you want them to do. The muscles push against the belt to increase pressure, but during times of high force production when you are not using a belt, you want the muscles to contract and pull in to increase intra-abdominal pressure. When the time comes to produce a large amount of force without a belt, the intra-abdominal pressure drops, which leaves the spine unprotected, increasing the chance of injury. Also, the use of a belt may strain the cardiovascular system by increasing blood pressure.

The natural supporting musculature of the body can also increase intra-abdominal pressure and protect the spine and lumbar regions. By using a belt, the core musculature of the body may not receive the necessary training stimulus, especially for strengthening the abdominal muscles. By doing strength exercises without a belt, all of the various muscle groups utilized in a given lift can be stimulated without relying on the support of the belt.

Using a belt is primarily beneficial when a person is training for a sport that requires maximal lifts. Never put the back at risk for injury if there are no performance gains to be made.

A weight lifting belt might be useful in protecting the back during periods of rehabilitation. During this time, you should not attempt maximum lifts but should be training to strengthen the entire body without risking further injury to the back.

The final decision on the use of belts can be made by answering the questions "What is the final goal of the program?" and "What is the person who is exercising trying to accomplish?"

DELAYED ONSET MUSCLE SORENESS

Many people, regardless of their fitness level, experience muscle soreness after engaging in strenuous exercise or at the beginning of a new exercise program. Many times the soreness and stiffness are not felt until twenty-four to forty-eight hours after the completion of the exercise. This type of muscle soreness is referred to as *delayed onset muscle soreness* (DOMS).

Physiological research reveals that the primary cause of DOMS is the overloading of a muscle during the eccentric (lengthening) portion of the movement. Greater tension can be generated during an eccentric action compared with either a concentric (shortening) or isometric (no movement) action. Thus the muscle cells become more susceptible to structural damage. This damage can lead to muscle soreness, decreased range of motion of the joint-lever system, a loss of strength, and a possible decrease in neuromuscular function.

Ways to prevent or lessen the effects of DOMS are as follows:

Warm-up

Warming up before an exercise prepares the body to exercise. Research data indicates that proper warm-up before eccentric exercise may be a sound method to alleviate DOMS. Using a warm-up set of lower resistance for each strength exercise will in most cases be very beneficial.

Repeated Bout Effect

Research has found that the musculature will adjust to the stress of exercise and become less susceptible to damage. One study found that even after one exercise bout, the inflammatory response to muscle damage was lessened when compared with engaging in the second bout of activity. It may be that the muscle cells become slightly longer so that the effects of the eccentric actions are less damaging. Another possibility is that the nervous system becomes more efficient in activating the muscle, which relieves the amount of stress on the active motor units.

The repeated bout effect can be facilitated when the first bout of exercise is only of a moderate intensity. If you engage in a program that produces little DOMS, an adaptation of the body will begin and the training process will be positive. In any strength training program you should start gradually and not make large increases in the overload of the selected exercises. Even well-trained individuals will develop DOMS if they make dramatically large increases or change the workout without a gradual adjustment to the program.

4 Body Measurements and Record Keeping

Attempting to reach the goal of strength development can be compared to taking a journey. If you are planning a trip, you need to know where you are starting from and how many miles you have traveled.

By taking your body measurements when you start your program, you will have a means to determine the progress you are making. Record keeping will enable you to evaluate how well the body responds to specific exercises and thus make any changes that might be beneficial to your individual needs. As you compare the increases in resistance used in the various exercises, you also will have a means to determine the strength gains being made by selected body parts.

TAKING MEASUREMENTS

One of the simplest methods to monitor change is to measure the circumference of selected body parts with a tape. When taking measurements, keep the tape firm, but do not apply enough pressure to make indentations in the skin. By following this procedure, you will have measurements that are reliable and indicate structural changes. All the measurements should be taken in a standing position. In some cases you may wish to take two sets of measurements, one with the body part relaxed and a second with the body part in a flexed position.

Following are some standardized procedures to follow in measuring selected body parts. Figure 4.1 can be used to record the body measurements.

Neck—measure at the smallest circumference when relaxed.

Shoulders—measure the circumference at the greatest width.

Chest—*relaxed,* measure at greatest circumference after exhaling; *flexed,* measure at greatest circumference after inhaling.

Upper Arm—*relaxed,* measure at largest circumference with arm hanging; *flexed,* measure at largest circumference with elbow at a 90° angle.

Forearm—*relaxed,* measure largest circumference with arm hanging; *flexed,* measure largest circumference while flexing muscles by bending the elbow and the wrist.

Waist—measure at smallest circumference after exhaling.

Name _____ Age _____

Date											
Body Weight											
Neck											
Shoulders											
Chest	Relaxed										
	Flexed										
Upper Arm											
Relaxed	Right										
	Left										
Flexed	Right										
	Left										
Forearm											
Relaxed	Right										
	Left										
Flexed	Right										
	Left										
Waist											
Hips											
Thigh											
Relaxed	Right										
	Left										
Flexed	Right										
	Left										
Calf											
Relaxed	Right										
	Left										
Flexed	Right										
	Left										
Other Body Parts											

Figure 4.1 Body Measurement Chart

Hips—measure at largest circumference.

Thigh—*relaxed,* measure the largest circumference; *flexed,* measure the largest circumference while straightening the leg and contracting the thigh muscles.

Calf—*relaxed,* measure the largest circumference; *flexed,* measure the largest circumference while contracting the muscles of the lower leg by raising the heel.

STRENGTH TEST

Although it may be impossible to determine the exact amount of force a given muscle group may exert, it is possible to estimate strength fitness rating by a series of strength tests. This information can be helpful in determining some body areas that might require more exercises to bring about positive results. Figure 4.2 contains the information and procedures to follow to complete the strength test.

STRENGTH TRAINING RECORD

Compiling a strength training record can also be a tremendous aid in your program. This record enables you to know the exercises you are using and the exact poundage to lift for that exercise. By comparing the various exercise days, you can easily determine how much improvement you have made at any given time. Figure 4.3 is an example of a strength training record.

THE SPORT EXPERIENCE

Use the body measurement chart, strength test, and strength training record to record your information at the start of your strength training program. After you have engaged in your training program for three or more months, take all of these measurements again to determine how your body is changing. Additional body measurement charts, strength tests, and strength training records can be found in Appendices A, B, and C.

PROCEDURES FOR ADMINISTERING STRENGTH TEST
1. Familiarize yourself with the six exercises utilized for the test.
   a. Lat Pull-down (LPD)—Start in a seated position and have someone hold the subject down at the shoulders. (page 99)
   b. Leg Extension (LE) (page 126)
   c. Bench Press (BP) (page 90)
   d. Curl-Up (CU)—Hold the weight on the front of the forehead, keep the knees flexed at a 100° angle, and have someone hold the feet. Curl forward and touch the elbows to the knees. (page 108)
   e. Leg Curl (LC)—flex the knee until the subject reaches a 90° angle. (page 141)
   f. Arm Curl (AC) (page 63)
2. Determine subject's weight in pounds.
3. Determine the amount of resistance to be used for each exercise. To obtain this number, multiply the body weight by the percentage of body weight given for each exercise in the chart at the bottom of the worksheet. Round the number to the lowest five pounds. For example, 54 is rounded to 50.
4. Record your resistance in the bottom of the worksheet.
5. Perform the maximum continuous number of repetitions for each exercise.
6. Determine the percentile rank for each exercise.

Strength Test													
Men							Women						
% Rank	LPD	LE	BP	CU	LC	AC	% Rank	LPD	LE	BP	CU	LC	AC
90	19	19	19	23	19	19	90	21	18	20	22	12	20
80	16	15	16	17	15	15	80	16	13	16	14	10	16
70	13	14	13	14	13	12	70	13	11	13	11	9	14
60	11	13	11	12	11	10	60	11	10	11	6	7	12
50	10	12	10	10	10	9	50	10	9	10	5	6	10
40	9	10	7	8	8	8	40	9	8	5	4	5	8
30	7	9	5	5	6	7	30	7	7	3	2	4	7
20	6	7	3	3	4	5	20	6	5	1	1	3	6
10	4	5	1	2	3	3	10	3	3	0	0	1	3
5	3	3	0	1	1	2	5	2	1	0	0	0	2

Adapted from the test developed by W. W. K. Hoeger and D. R. Hopkins and used with their permission.

Figure 4.2 Strength Test

7. Determine the strength category and number of points for each exercise.

% Rank	90	80–89	60–79	40–59	20–39	10–19	less than 10
Strength Category	Superior	Excellent	Good	Average	Fair	Poor	Very Poor
Points	19	17	15	13	11	9	7

8. Record percentile rank, strength category, and number of points below.

Exercise	% Body Weight		Resistance	Reps	% Rank	Strength Category	Pts
	Men	Women					
1. Lat Pull-Down	.70	.45					
2. Leg Extension	.65	.50					
3. Bench Press	.75	.45					
4. Curl-Up	.16	.10					
5. Leg Curl	.32	.25					
6. Arm Curl	.35	.18					
						Total Points	

Figure 4.2 Strength Test–Continued

Name _____ Age _____

Date					
Exercise	Wt Reps	Wt Reps	Wt Reps	Wt Reps	Wt Reps

Figure 4.3   Strength Training Record

5

Planning the Strength Training Program

MAJOR HUMAN MUSCLES

Familiarity with basic anatomy and various movements of the human body is helpful in designing weight training programs. Figure 5.1 contains a diagram of the major human muscles, and table 5.1 lists the name of the muscle, the action of the muscle, and the sport in which the muscle is used. By using this information, you can analyze a sport to determine the most important movements and the muscles involved. For example, muscle no. 26, the trapezius, tilts the head back, elevates the shoulder point, and adducts the scapula. This muscle is used in the wrestler's bridge, passing a football, and cleaning a barbell, as well as in the breaststroke, archery, and batting.

Figure 5.1 Major Human Muscles

Table 5.1   Muscle Action and Sport Use

Supinate: rotate forearm to palms-up
Invert: turn sole of foot inward
Evert: turn sole of foot outward
Elevate: raise a part against gravity
Depress: lower a part, yielding to gravity
Lateral: located toward the outer side
Medial: located toward the middle
Flex: bend at a joint, decreasing angle

Extend: straighten at a joint
Adduct: move toward midline of body
Abduct: move away from midline
Rotate: move part around an axis
Prone: face downward
Supine: face upward
Pronate: rotate forearm to palms-down

Muscle	Primary Action (numbers in parentheses indicate muscles that assist)	Sport in Which Greatest Resistance Is Encountered
1. Flexor digitorum-profundus 2. Extensor digitorum 3. Flexor pollicis longus 4. Extensor pollicis longus 5. Abductor pollicis longus 6. Adductor pollicis longus	Flexes fingers Extends fingers Flexes thumb Extends thumb Abducts thumb Adducts and flexes thumb	Any sport in which one grasps an opponent, partner, or equipment, such as wrestling, hand-to-hand balancing, tennis, horizontal bar, ball bat, etc.
7. Flexor carpi radialis 8. Flexor carpi ulnaris	Flexes wrist palmward (8), abducts hand (9) Flexes wrist palmward (7), adducts hand (10)	Tennis, throwing a baseball, passing a football, handball, ring work, two-handed pass in basketball, batting, golf swing
9. Extensor carpi radialis longus and brevis 10. Extensor carpi ulnaris	Extends wrist (10), abducts hand (7) Extends wrist (9), adducts hand (8)	Backhand stroke in tennis and badminton, Olympic weight lifting, bait and fly casting
11. Pronator teres 12. Pronator quadratus	Pronates forearm	Tennis forehand, shot put, throwing a punch, throwing a baseball, passing a football
13. Supinator	Supinates forearm (16)	Throwing a curve ball, batting, fencing thrust
14. Biceps brachii 15. Brachialis	Flexes forearm (16)	Ring work, rope climb, archery, pole vaulting, wrestling, backstroke in swimming
16. Brachioradialis	Flexes forearm, supinates forearm	Rowing, cleaning a barbell, rope climb
17. Triceps brachii 18. Anconeus	Extends forearm	Breaststroke, shot put, parallel bar work, vaulting, hand shivers in football, hand balancing, batting pole vaulting, fencing thrust, passing, boxing

Continued.

Table 5.1   Muscle Action and Sport Use–Continued

Muscle	Primary Action (numbers in parentheses indicate muscles that assist)	Sport in Which Greatest Resistance Is Encountered

19. Deltoid
    Anterior fibers
    Posterior fibers
20. Supraspinatus
21. Infraspinatus
22. Teres minor
	Abducts humerus (20)
	    Flexes humerus
	    Extends humerus
	Abducts humerus (19)
	Rotates humerus laterally
		Hand balancing, canoeing, shot put, pole vaulting, tennis, archery, batting, fencing thrust, passing a football, tackling, breaststroke, back and crawl strokes, golf swing, handball

23. Teres major	Adducts, extends, and rotates humerus medially (32)	Rope climb, canoe racing, ring work, rowing, batting, crawl, back, breast, and butterfly strokes, pole vaulting, golf
24. Pectoralis major	Adducts, flexes, and rotates humerus	Tackling, crawl, and backstrokes, tennis, passing a football, throwing a baseball, javelin, pole vaulting, wrestling, shot put, discus throw, straight-arm lever position in gymnastics, punching
25. Sternocleidomastoid	Flexes and laterally flexes neck, rotates head (27)	Crawl stroke, tucking chin in wrestling, football, boxing, distance running (breathing)
26. Trapezius	Bends head laterally toward shoulder Elevates shoulder Adducts scapula	Wrestler's bridge Passing a football, cleaning a barbell, breaststroke Archery, batting, breaststroke
27. Splenius cervicis/capitus	Extends head back Extends head (26) Rotates head	
28. Major and minor rhomboids, levator scapulae	Adducts and rotates scapula medially, depresses shoulder	Tennis backhand, batting, back and breaststroke
29. Subscapularis	Rotates humerus medially (24), stabilizes humerus in glenoid cavity to prevent displacement	Tackling, crawl and backstrokes, tennis, passing a football, throwing a baseball, javelin, pole vaulting, wrestling, shot put, discus throw, straight-arm level position in gymnastics

Continued.

| Table 5.1 | Muscle Action and Sport Use–Continued |

Muscle	Primary Action (numbers in parentheses indicate muscles that assist)	Sport in Which Greatest Resistance Is Encountered
30. Serratus anterior	Abducts scapula	Shot put, discus throw, tennis, archery, tackling, crawl stroke, passing a basketball, passing a football, punching
31. Erector spinae	Extends vertebral column	Discus and hammer throw, batting, golf swing, racing start in swimming, diving and tumbling, rowing, blocking in football
32. Latissimus dorsi	Adducts, extends, and rotates humerus medially; depresses shoulder	Rope climb, canoe racing, ring work, rowing, batting, crawl, back, breast, and butterfly strokes, pole vaulting, golf swing
33. Quadratus lumborum	Flexes vertebral column, flexes vertebral column laterally	The importance of this group in all sports, posture, and general fitness and appearance cannot be overstated
34. External abdominal oblique 35. Internal abdominal oblique	Flexes and rotates vertebral column	The importance of this group in all sports, posture, and general fitness and appearance cannot be overstated
36. Rectus abdominus 37. Transverse abdominus	Flexes vertebral column (33) Compresses abdomen	
38. Iliopsoas, pectineus	Flexes femur (42)	Running, hurdling, pole vaulting, kicking a football, line play, flutter kick, pike and tuck positions in diving and tumbling
39. Gluteus medius	Abducts femur, rotates femur medially	Hurdling, fencing, frog kick, shot put, running, line play, skating
40. Gluteus maximus 41. Tensor fasciae	Extends femur, rotates femur laterally Flexes, abducts, and rotates femur medially	Skiing, shot put, running, quick starts in track, all jumping and skipping, line play, skating, swimming start, changing directions while running
42. Rectus femoris 43. Vastus medialis 44. Vastus lateralis 45. Sartorius	Extends lower leg (43, 44), flexes femur Extends lower leg Flexes lower leg, flexes femur, rotates femur laterally	Skiing, skating, quick starts, all jumping, kick in football or soccer, flutter kick, frog kick, water skiing, diving, trampoline and tumbling, bicycling, catching in baseball

Continued.

| Table 5.1 | Muscle Action and Sport Use–Continued |

Muscle	Primary Action (numbers in parentheses indicate muscles that assist)	Sport in Which Greatest Resistance Is Encountered
46. Adductor magnus	Adducts femur (48)	Skiing, skating, frog kick, broken field running, bareback horseback riding
47. Adductor longus		
48. Gracilis	Adducts femur, flexes lower leg	
49. Biceps femoris	Flexes lower leg, rotates lower leg laterally (53, 54); extends femur (48, 50, 51)	Skiing, skating, quick starts in track and swimming, hurdling line play, all jumping
50. Semimembranosus	Flexes lower leg, rotates lower leg medially (52)	
51. Semitendinosus	Extends femur	
52. Popliteus	Flexes lower leg, rotates lower leg medially	
53. Plantaris	Plantar flexes foot (when knee is almost straight)	Quick starts in track, swimming, basketball, football, skating, all jumping, skiing
54. Gastrocnemius	Flexes lower leg	
55. Soleus	Plantar flexes foot	
56. Peroneus longus	Plantar flexes and everts foot	Changing directions while running, skating, skiing, running, all jumping, racing starts, skating turns
57. Peroneus brevis		
58. Extensor digitorum	Extends the four smaller toes	
59. Extensor hallicus	Extends the big toe	
60. Tibialis anterior	Dorsiflexes and inverts foot	
61. Tibialis posterior	Plantar flexes and inverts foot	
62. Flexor digitorum longus	Flexes the four smaller toes	
63. Flexor hallicus longus	Flexes the big toe	

Source: Adapted from Muscle Action Chart by Cramer Products, Inc. Reprinted by permission of Cramer Products, Inc., P.O. Box 1001, Gardner, KS 66030.

BODY PARTS METHOD

A more practical approach in writing a strength program, especially for those individuals just starting a beginning program, is to use a body parts approach.

By including these body parts a majority of all of the muscles in the body will be exercised and increase in strength.

In planning a strength training program to ensure overall body strength and development, six major body parts should be included:

1. Neck
2. Arms (biceps, triceps, wrists, and shoulders)

3. Chest
4. Back
5. Midsection
6. Legs (front and back)

When designing the program, the individual must be aware of the equipment available and the amount of training time that he or she has. The desired outcomes to be achieved by the program should also be known.

At the end of this chapter are descriptions of the various exercises that can be employed. Photographs show the exercise, followed by an explanation concerning the starting position of the exercise, the action to be followed, and any precautions to be aware of while doing the exercise.

Figures 5.2, A–J lists the six major body parts and the exercises that will strengthen the muscles in these body parts. Also listed is the page number where the description of the exercise is found. By using these figures you can select exercises to develop any part of the body. Please note that although an exercise is listed under one area, as the bench press is under the chest area, it will also involve other parts of the body such as the arms.

FIGURE 5.2 A, NECK

Body Part	Exercise	Page
Neck	Partner resistance	62

FIGURE 5.2 B, BICEPS

Body Part	Exercise	Page
Biceps	Arm curl	63
	Reverse curl	64
	Preacher-board curl	65
	Dumbbell curl	66
	Incline dumbbell curl	67
	Dumbbell concentration curl	68
	Supine curl	69

FIGURE 5.2 C, TRICEPS

Body Part	Exercise	Page
Triceps	Seated overhead press	70
	Behind-neck press	71
	Seated behind-neck press	72
	Standing dumbbell press	73
	Seated dumbbell press	74
	Lying barbell triceps extension	75
	Standing barbell triceps extension	76
	Lying dumbbell triceps extension	77
	Seated dumbbell triceps extension	78
	Dumbbell kickback	79
	Triceps press-down	80

FIGURE 5.2 D, WRISTS

Body Part	Exercise	Page
Wrists	Wrist curl	81
	Reverse wrist curl	82
	Dumbbell wrist curl	83
	Reverse dumbbell wrist curl	84
	Wrist roller	85

FIGURE 5.2 E, SHOULDERS

Body Part	Exercise	Page
Shoulders	Upright rowing	86
	Side lateral raise	87
	Dips	88
	Seated dips	89

FIGURE 5.2 F, CHEST

Body Part	Exercise	Page
Chest	Barbell bench press	90
	Dumbbell bench press	91
	Barbell incline bench press	92
	Dumbbell incline bench press	93
	Bench flys	94
	Bent-arm flys	95
	Decline press	96
	Bent-arm pullover	97

FIGURE 5.2 G, BACK

Body Part	Exercise	Page
Back	Pull-up	98
	Lat pull-down	99
	Bent-over rowing	100
	Dumbbell bent-over rowing	101
	Seated rowing	102
	Dead lift	103
	Good morning	104
	Back raise	105
	Shrugs	106
	Bent-over lateral raise	107

FIGURE 5.2 H, MIDSECTION

Body Part	Exercise	Page
Midsection	Curl-up	108
	V-sit	109
	Roman chair curl-up	110
	Hanging knee-up	111
	Sitting knee-up	112
	Side bend	113
	Twists	114
	Crunches	115
	High Pulley Crunches	116
	Machine Crunches	117
	Incline Bench Sit-up	118
	Roman Chair Side Bends	119

FIGURE 5.2 I, LEGS–FRONT

Body Part	Exercise	Page
Legs–Front	Leg splits	120
	Toe raise	121
	Front leg kick	122
	Side leg kick	123
	Leg press	124
	Vertical leg press	125
	Leg extension	126
	Bench jump	127
	Lunge squat	128
	Hack squat	129
	Trap bar	130
	Back squat	131
	Front squat	132
	Hang clean	133
	Power clean	135

FIGURE 5.2 J, LEGS–BACK

Body Part	Exercise	Page
Legs–Back	Standing heel raise	137
	Single-heel raise	138
	Sitting heel raise	139
	Toe extension	140
	Leg curl	141
	Glute-ham raise	142

DESIGNING A STRENGTH TRAINING PROGRAM

You can now design a program using one or more exercises per body part. The resistance to be used in this program would be determined by using the "guesstimate" method, which was explained in chapter 3.

If a person wishes to emphasize a specific body part, then more than one exercise could be chosen to insure a greater change.

Page in Text	Body Part	Exercise	Sets	Repetitions	Rest Interval
90	Chest	1. Barbell Bench Press	3	10 RM	2 minutes
108	Midsection	2. Curl-up	3	30 RM	2 minutes
80	Triceps	3. Triceps press-down	3	10 RM	2 minutes
124	Legs	4. Leg press	3	10 RM	2 minutes
88	Shoulders	5. Dips	3	10 RM	2 minutes
62	Neck	6. Partner resistance	3	10 RM	2 minutes
63	Biceps	7. Arm curl	3	10 RM	2 minutes
141	Legs	8. Leg curl	3	10 RM	2 minutes
99	Back	9. Lat pull-down	3	10 RM	2 minutes
81	Wrists	10. Wrist curl	3	10 RM	2 minutes

Note that the rest period for each exercise is two minutes. If you find that the time allotted for strength training is too short to do all of the exercises, then an excellent routine to follow is to alternate the selected exercises in groups of two rather than taking a rest period. For example, first you do one set of the bench press and then one set of curl-ups, then do another set of the bench press and a second set of curl-ups, and so on. You combine exercises 1 and 2, 3 and 4, 5 and 6, 7 and 8, and 9 and 10. Since you are using different muscle groups, recovery can take place in the nonexercising muscle group while you are training the exercising muscle group.

As explained in chapter 3, it is possible to obtain strength gains by using one set for each exercise and not having a recovery period between each of the exercises. This is another way to reduce the time needed for a strength training program.

THE SPORT EXPERIENCE

Write a beginning strength training program for yourself using the strength training worksheet found in Appendix D.

STRENGTH TRAINING EXERCISES

Recall that the overload principle is what brings about the desired changes in a strength training program, not the training device utilized in the program. For example, if you do an arm curl with either free weights or a machine and use the proper overload, you will obtain a training effect.

NECK

Partner Resistance

Starting Position: Take a seated position on the bench.

Action: To provide resistance, the partner pushes against the head as the neck muscles contract in the various positions: forward, backward, and sideways.

Precautions: Be sure to exercise all the neck muscles. Do not jerk the head in the movement.

Arm Curl

Starting Position: Grasp the bar about the width of the shoulders using a palms-up grip. The arms are extended, and the bar rests against the thighs.

Action: Curl the bar up to the shoulder area. Touch, and then return to the starting position.

Precautions: The elbows should be kept close to the sides of the body. Keep the body erect with the head up. Avoid any unnecessary body movement.

Reverse Curl

Starting Position: Grasp the bar about the width of the shoulders using a palms-down grip. The arms are extended, and the bar rests against the thighs.

Action: Curl the bar up to the shoulder area. Touch, and then return to the starting position.

Precautions: The elbows should be kept close to the sides of the body. Keep the body erect with the head up. Avoid any unnecessary body movement.

BICEPS

Preacher-Board Curl

Starting Position: Adjust the stand to a height where you can place your arms over the angled padding with the back of the arms resting on the pad. Grasp the bar about the width of the shoulders using a palms-up grip.

Action: Curl the bar up to the shoulder area. Touch, and then return to the starting position.

Precautions: Do not jerk the weight, and avoid any unnecessary body movement.

Dumbbell Curl

Starting Position: Stand erect with the feet about shoulder width. Grasp the dumbbells with a palms-up grip with the arms fully extended.

Action: Curl the dumbbells until they reach the top of the shoulders. Touch and return to the starting position.

Precautions: Keep the elbows close to the body. Do not jerk or use any unnecessary motion in the movement.

NOTE: This exercise can be performed in a seated position and can also be done by alternating one arm then the other in the curling movement.

BICEPS

Incline Dumbbell Curl

Starting Position: Lie on an incline board while grasping the dumbbells in a palms-up grip. The arms are extended with the head and back against the board.

Action: Curl the dumbbells until they reach the shoulders. Touch, and return to the starting position.

Precautions: Do not arch the back or use the legs in the movement. Do not jerk the weight to start the motion.

Dumbbell Concentration Curl

Starting Position: Take a seated position on the bench. Grasp the dumbbell in the palms-up grip, and place the elbow on the inside of the right thigh to stabilize the upper arm. The arm is fully extended. The left hand is placed on the left thigh for support.

Action: Curl the dumbbell to the shoulder. Touch, and return to the starting position. After completing the desired number of repetitions, change the dumbbell to the left hand to complete the exercise for both arms.

Precautions: Keep the upper torso and legs stationary during the exercise. Do not jerk the dumbbell, and avoid any unnecessary motion during the movement.

BICEPS

Supine Curl

Starting Position: Lie on the bench with the feet flat on the floor. Grasp the dumbbells with a palms-up grip. The arms are extended from the sides of the body toward the floor.

Action: Curl the dumbbells to the shoulders. Touch, and return to the starting position.

Precautions: Do not arch the back or use any unnecessary motion during the movement.

Seated Overhead Press

Starting Position: Take a seat on the bench with the feet flat on the floor. Use a palms-up grip with the bar placed at the top of the chest. The head is up and the back straight.

Action: Push the bar overhead until the arms are fully extended. Return to the starting position.

Precautions: Do not jerk the weight or use any unnecessary body motion in the movement.

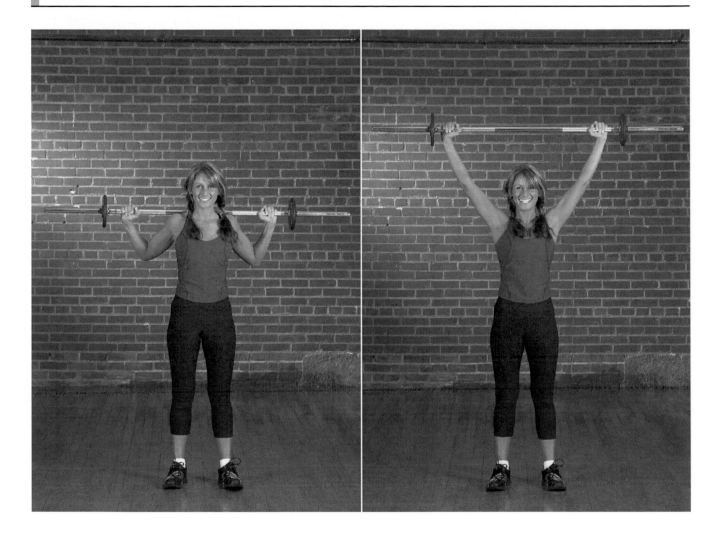

Behind-Neck Press

Starting Position: Stand erect with the feet shoulder width apart. The head is up with the eyes facing straight ahead. The bar is behind the neck and across the shoulders and held with an overhand grip.

Action: Push the bar overhead until the arms are fully extended. Lower the bar to the starting position.

Precautions: Keep the body erect during exercise. Do not bend the knees to assist the upper-body muscles in the movement.

Seated Behind-Neck Press

Starting Position: Take a seat on the bench with the feet flat on the floor. The head is up with the eyes facing straight ahead. The bar is behind the neck and across the shoulders and held with an overhand grip.

Action: Push the bar overhead until the arms are fully extended. Lower the bar to the starting position.

Precautions: Do not jerk the weight or use any unnecessary body motion during the movement.

Standing Dumbbell Press

Starting Position: Stand erect with the feet shoulder width apart. Grasp the dumbbells with the palms facing forward, and elbows level with shoulders.

Action: Push the dumbbell overhead until the arms are fully extended. Lower the dumbbells to the starting position.

Precautions: Do not jerk the dumbbells or bend the knees to assist in the movement. Keep the body erect during the motion.

Seated Dumbbell Press

Starting Position: Take a seat on the bench with the feet flat on the floor. Grasp the dumbbells, and bring them to the shoulders with the palms facing forward.

Action: Push the dumbbells overhead until the arms are fully extended. Lower the dumbbells to the starting position.

Precautions: Do not jerk the dumbbells or use any unnecessary body motion in the movement.

NOTE: This exercise can also be performed by alternating one arm then the other in the pressing movement.

TRICEPS

Lying Barbell Triceps Extension

Starting Position: Lie flat on the bench with the feet flat on the floor. Grasp the bar with a narrow overhand grip so that the hands are about six inches or less apart. The arms are fully extended above the chest.

Action: Keep the upper arms extended, and lower the bar until it touches the forehead. Return to the starting position.

Precautions: Do not arch the body or allow the elbows to flare out to the sides during the movement.

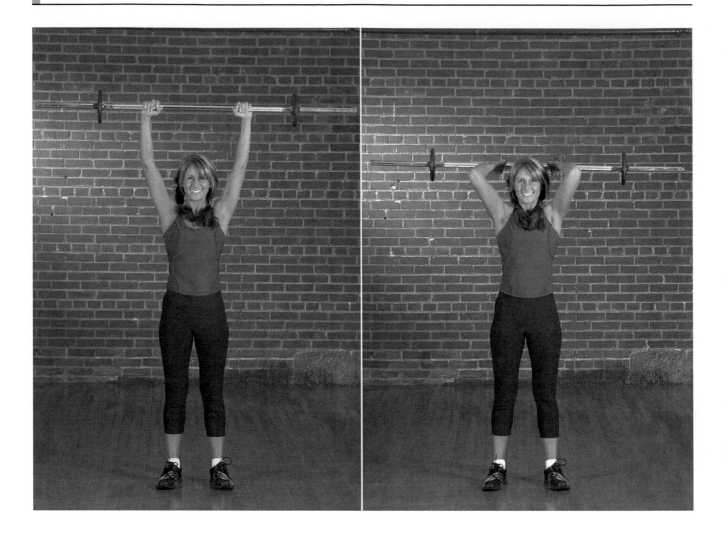

Standing Barbell Triceps Extension

Starting Position: Stand erect with the feet shoulder width apart. Grasp the bar with a narrow overhand grip so that the hands are about 12 inches apart. The arms are fully extended above the head.

Action: Keep the lower arms stationary, and lower the bar until it is back of the head. Return to the starting position.

Precautions: Do not jerk the weight or bend the knees to assist in the lift. Keep the elbows in as much as possible during the movement.

NOTE: This exercise can also be performed in a seated position.

TRICEPS

Lying Dumbbell Triceps Extension

Starting Position: Lie flat on the bench with the feet flat on the floor. Grasp the dumbbell in both hands with the fingers interlaced. The arms are fully extended above the chest.

Action: Keep the upper arms extended, and lower the dumbbell until it touches the back of the head. Return to the starting position.

Precautions: Do not arch the body or allow the elbows to flare out to the sides during the movement.

Seated Dumbbell Triceps Extension

Starting Position: Take a seat on the bench with the feet flat on the floor. Grasp the dumbbell in both hands with the fingers interlaced. The arms are fully extended above the head.

Action: Keep the upper arms extended, and lower the dumbbell until it touches the back of the neck. Return to the starting position.

Precautions: Do not jerk the dumbbell or allow the elbows to flare out to the sides during the movement.

NOTE: Dumbbell triceps extensions can also be done in a standing position, or the exercise can be performed using a dumbbell held in one hand at a time.

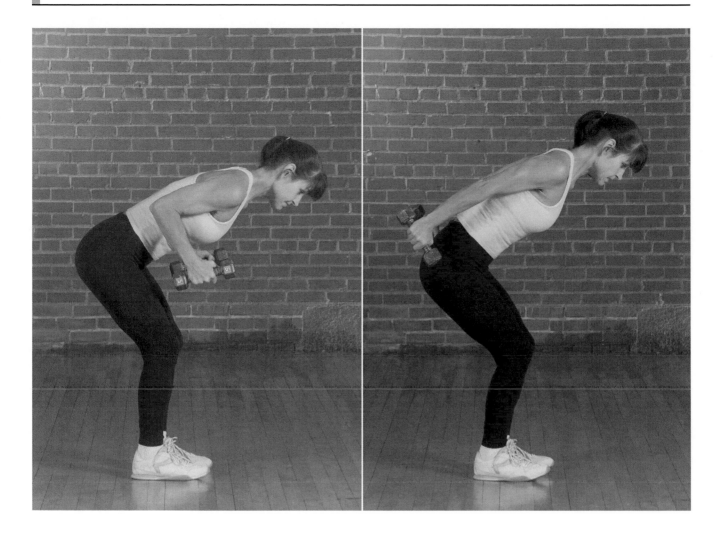

Dumbbell Kickback

Starting Position: Bend over at the waist until the upper torso is almost parallel to the floor. The feet are shoulder width apart. Grasp the dumbbells in both hands so that the palms are facing each other. The upper arms are almost parallel to the floor, and the forearms are bent at a 90° angle to the upper arms.

Action: Straighten both arms to the back until the elbows lock. Return to the starting position.

Precautions: Keep the body stationary, and do not jerk the dumbbells in the movement.

Triceps Press-Down

Starting Position: Stand erect with the feet shoulder width apart. Grasp the bar of the machine with a palms-down grip with the hands about six inches apart. The bar is chest height.

Action: Keep the upper arms stationary, and push the bar to the thighs by extending the forearms. Touch, and return to the starting position.

Precautions: Lean slightly in toward the bar while doing the exercise. Do not move the body to assist the triceps in extending the bar. Keep the elbows close to the body.

WRISTS

Wrist Curl

Starting Position: Take a seat on the bench with the feet flat on the floor. Grasp the bar with a palms-up grip, and support the arms on the thighs with the wrists extended beyond the knees. The wrists are relaxed so the bar is as low to the floor as possible.

Action: Curl the weight upward as high as possible without moving the forearms. Return to the starting position.

Precautions: Do not jerk the weight, and make sure that only the wrists move during the exercise.

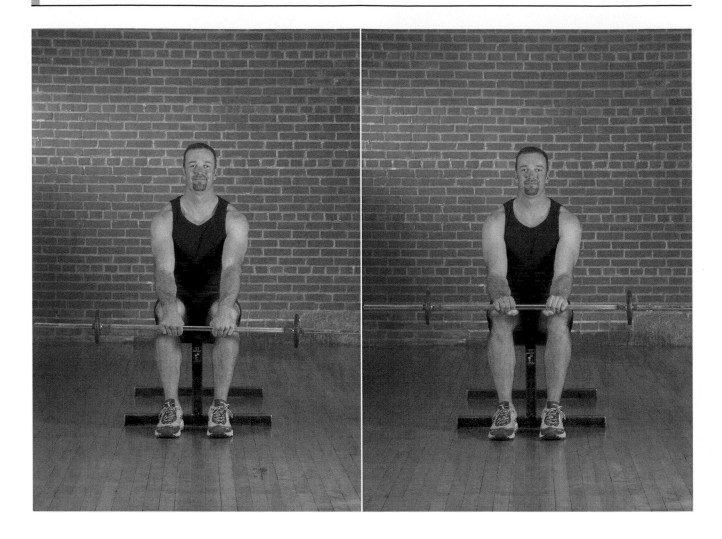

Reverse Wrist Curl

Starting Position: Take a seat on the bench with the feet flat on the floor. Grasp the bar with a palms-down grip, and support the arms on the thighs with the wrists extended beyond the knees. The wrists are relaxed so the bar is as low to the floor as possible.

Action: Curl the weight upward as high as possible without moving the forearms. Return to the starting position.

Precautions: Do not jerk the weight, and make sure that only the wrists move during the exercise.

Dumbbell Wrist Curl

Starting Position: Take a seat on the bench with the feet flat on the floor. Grasp the dumbbell in each hand with a palms-up grip, and support the arms on the thighs with the wrists extended beyond the knees. The wrists are relaxed so the dumbbells are as low to the floor as possible.

Action: Curl the dumbbells upward as high as possible without moving the forearms. Return to the starting position.

Precautions: Do not jerk the weight, and make sure that only the wrists move during the exercise.

Reverse Dumbbell Wrist Curl

Starting Position: Take a seat on the bench with the feet flat on the floor. Grasp the dumbbell in each hand with a palms-down grip, and support the arms on the thighs with the wrists extended beyond the knees. The wrists are relaxed so the dumbbells are as low to the floor as possible.

Action: Curl the dumbbells upward as high as possible without moving the forearms. Return to the starting position.

Precautions: Do not jerk the weight, and make sure that only the wrists move during the exercise.

Wrist Roller

Starting Position: Stand erect with the feet about shoulder width apart. Grasp the bar with a palms-down grip with the hands approximately eight inches apart. The wrist roller consists of a weight attached to a bar by a three-foot length of rope. The arms are extended forward and parallel to the floor.

Action: Rotate the hands about the bar until all of the rope is wrapped around the bar. Return to the starting position.

Precautions: Do not move the body to assist in the movement, and do not allow the weight to drop on the extension because this could burn the hands.

NOTE: A clockwise rotation develops the wrist flexors, and a counter-clockwise rotation develops the wrist extensors.

Upright Rowing

Starting Position: Stand erect with the feet about shoulder width apart. Grasp the bar with a palms-down grip with the hands about two inches apart. The arms are extended so the bar rests against the thighs.

Action: Keep the head up and the chest high. Raise the bar until it touches the chin. Return to the starting position.

Precautions: Do not move the body to assist in the exercise. Keep the bar close to the body with the elbows higher than the hands, and don't jerk to start the movement.

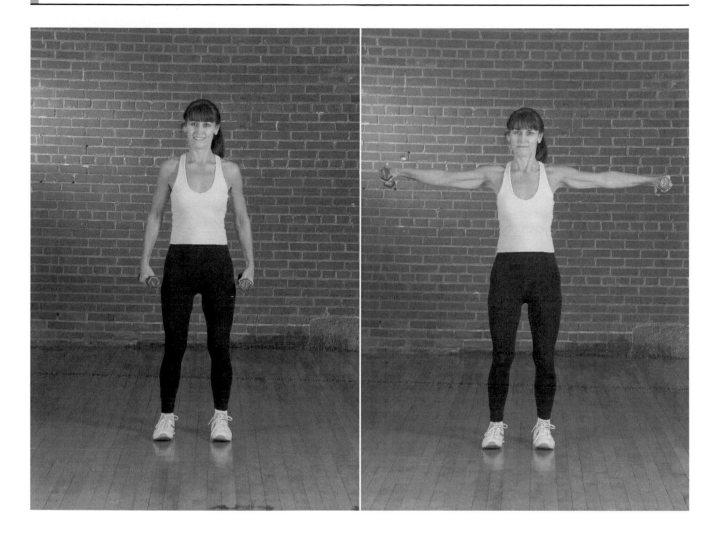

Side Lateral Raise

Starting Position: Stand erect with the feet about shoulder width apart. Grasp a dumbbell in each hand using an overhand grip. The arms are extended downward in front of the body.

Action: Raise the dumbbells upward to the sides of the body until the elbows lock and the arms are approximately parallel to the floor. Return to the starting position.

Precautions: Keep the body stationary, and do not jerk the dumbbells in the movement.

NOTE: You can vary the hand grip. As you change the palms from downward to upward, resistance is moved from the medial deltoid to the anterior deltoid.

Dips

Starting Position: The body is supported in a suspended position between the parallel bars with the arms fully extended.

Action: Dip downward as far as possible. Return to the starting position.

Precautions: Avoid unnecessary body swing in the movement. Add weights to the body to increase the resistance, if needed.

NOTE: If it is not possible to do the dip as described, the resistance can be decreased as shown in the following pictures.

Seated Dips

Starting Position: The body is supported on two benches by placing the feet on one bench and the hands on the other. The arms are fully extended, and the back is straight.

Action: Bend the arms, and allow the body to lower as far as possible. Return to the starting position.

Precautions: Avoid unnecessary body movement in performing the exercise. Weights can be placed on the upper thighs to increase the resistance, if needed.

Barbell Bench Press

Starting Position: Lie flat on the bench with the knees bent and feet flat on the floor. Use a palms-up grip, approximately the width of the shoulders. Hold the bar in a chest-rest position.

Action: Press the bar directly upward until elbows lock, and then return to the starting position.

Precautions: Do not arch the back or raise the buttocks during movement. Do not bounce the weight off the chest.

NOTE: This exercise can be done using a narrow grip to increase resistance to the triceps.

Dumbbell Bench Press

Starting Position: Lie flat on the bench with the knees bent and feet flat on the floor. Grasp the dumbbells with a palms-up grip. Hold the dumbbells in a chest-rest position.

Action: Press the dumbbells directly upward until elbows lock, and return to the starting position.

Precautions: Do not arch the back or raise the buttocks during movement. Keep the elbows away from the body and pointed outward.

Barbell Incline Bench Press

Starting Position: Sit on inclined bench with feet flat against the floor. Use a palms-up grip, approximately the width of the shoulders. Hold the bar in a chest-rest position.

Action: Press the bar upward until elbows lock, and then return to the starting position.

Precautions: Do not arch the back or raise the buttocks during movement. Do not bounce weight off the chest.

Dumbbell Incline Bench Press

Starting Position: Sit on inclined bench with feet flat against the floor. Grasp the dumbbells with a palms-up grip, with elbows level with shoulders.

Action: Press the dumbbells upward until the elbows lock, and then return to the starting position.

Precautions: Do not arch the back or raise the buttocks during the movement. Keep the elbows away from the body and pointed outward.

Bench Flys

Starting Position: Lie flat on bench. Hold dumbbell in each hand, straight up over the chest with the palms inward.

Action: Lower the dumbbells with the arms straight until the arms are parallel to the floor, and then return to the starting position.

Precautions: Do not arch the back or raise the buttocks. Lower and raise the dumbbells slowly.

Bent-Arm Flys

Starting Position: Lie flat on bench. Hold a dumbbell in each hand with the arms extended over the chest in a semiflexed position.

Action: Lower the dumbbells with the arms semiflexed, as far as they can go toward the floor. Return to the starting position.

Precautions: Keep the arms semiflexed. Do not arch the back or raise the buttocks. Lower and raise the dumbbells slowly.

Decline Press

Starting Position: Lie back on a 30° decline bench with the head at the lower end. Use a palms-up grip approximately the width of the shoulder. Hold the bar in a chest-rest position.

Action: Press the bar upward at approximately 60° until elbows lock, and then return to the starting position.

Precautions: Do not arch the back or raise the buttocks during movement. Do not bounce the weight off the chest.

CHEST

Bent-Arm Pullover

Starting Position: Lie flat on bench with knees bent and feet flat on the floor. Allow head to hang over the end of the bench. Use a palms-up grip with the hands approximately twelve inches apart. Hold the bar in a chest-rest position.

Action: Lower the bar back overhead as far as possible with the elbows bent. Pull the weight back to the starting position.

Precautions: Keep elbows close to the head and pointing toward the ceiling during the exercise. Avoid unnecessary arching of back. Do not jerk or make unnecessary body movements. Keep the bar close to face during the exercise movement.

Pull-Up

Starting Position: Use a palms-down grip, approximately the width of the shoulders, with arms extended to support body suspended from the bar.

Action: Pull body upward to the bar as high as possible, and then return to the starting position.

Precautions: Straighten out arms on each repetition. Avoid unnecessary body swing and movement. Add weights to body to increase the resistance, if needed.

NOTE: If you cannot do the pull-up as described, it is possible to decrease the resistance as shown in the second set of pictures.

Lat Pull-Down

Starting Position: Start in a seated position. Grasp the bar in a wide, palms-down grip with the arms fully extended.

Action: Pull the bar down until the bar is in front of the upper chest and then return to the starting position.

Precautions: Keep the upper body straight. Do not jerk or raise the body to assist in the movement.

NOTE: The same exercise can be done with the bar pulled downward behind the head.

Bent-Over Rowing

Starting Position: Start in a bent-over position with the upper torso parallel to the floor. The feet are shoulder width apart with the knees slightly bent. Grasp the bar with an overhand grip with the arms fully extended.

Action: Pull the bar upward until it touches the rib cage, and then return to the starting position.

Precautions: Keep the spine in an arched position to take pressure off the lower back. Do not jerk the weight or raise the body to assist in the movement.

Dumbbell Bent-Over Rowing

Starting Position: Start in a bent-over position with the upper torso parallel to the floor. The outside foot is on the floor with the knee slightly bent. Grasp the dumbbell with the arm fully extended, the opposite arm and leg supporting the body by contacting a bench for stability.

Action: Pull the dumbbell upward until it touches the torso, and then return to the starting position.

Precautions: Keep the elbow close to the body while doing the exercise. Do not jerk the weight or raise the body to assist in the movement.

Seated Rowing

Starting Position: Take a seated position with the legs fully extended and braced against the machine. Grasp the bar with a palms-down grip and the arms extended.

Action: Pull the bar toward the body until it touches the lower chest, and then return to the starting position.

Precautions: Keep the back straight during the exercise. Do not jerk to assist in the movement.

NOTE: This exercise can be done with a palms-up grip, which will utilize the biceps of the arm to a greater amount.

Dead Lift

Starting Position: Stand next to the bar with the front of legs touching the bar and the feet shoulder width apart. Bend down and grasp the bar with the palms facing toward the legs and the hands about shoulder width apart. Bend the legs with the hips lowered and head up. Arch the back to take stress off the lower back.

Action: Pull the bar up along the legs until the body is upright and the bar is on the front of the thighs. Then return to the starting position.

Precautions: Keep the bar close to the legs to reduce back strain. Always keep the head up and lift with the legs.

Good Morning

Starting Position: Stand with the bar behind the neck and resting on the shoulders. The feet are shoulder width apart with the legs straight.

Action: Bend forward at the waist until the upper torso is parallel with the floor, and then return to the starting position.

Precautions: Since this exercise puts stress on the lower back muscles, it is important to start with light resistance at first. Keep the head up at all times, and do not jerk to assist in the movement.

Back Raise

Starting Position: Take a prone position on the machine with the lower part of the body on the machine and the upper torso bent forward over the machine. The hands are interlocked behind the neck. It may be necessary to have a partner support the lower body by pushing down on the legs.

Action: Raise the upper torso upward until the body is parallel to the floor, and then return to the starting position.

Precautions: Do not hyperextend the back by going above parallel. Do not jerk or use any unnecessary motion to assist in the movement.

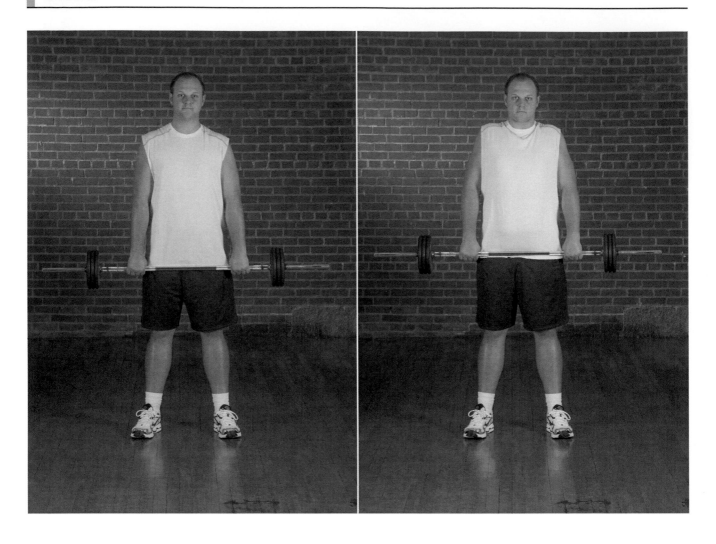

Shrugs

Starting Position: Stand upright and grasp the bar with a palms-down grip with the arms fully extended.

Action: Elevate the shoulder girdle as high as possible, and then return to the starting position.

Precautions: Keep the body straight, and do not bend the arms when raising the weight.

Bent-Over Lateral Raise

Starting Position: Start in a bent-over position with the upper torso parallel to the floor. The feet are shoulder width apart with the knees slightly bent. Grasp the dumbbells in each hand with the arms fully extended.

Action: Raise the dumbbells lateral from the body until the arms are parallel to the floor, and then return to the starting position.

Precautions: Keep the head up, and do not jerk the weight or raise the body to assist in the movement.

Curl-Up

Starting Position: Lie flat on the floor with legs bent at the knees and the feet flat on the floor. The hands are folded over the chest.

Action: Curl up to approximately a 30° angle. Rotate the right side of body toward left knee, and return to the starting position. On the next repetition rotate body toward right knee.

Precautions: Do not stabilize the feet unless absolutely necessary. Do not arch the back during the exercise, and keep the arms flat against the chest. Be sure to start by bending the head forward and progressively curl up to the 30° angle. Curl back to the starting position by touching lower back, upper back, and finally the head. A good check is to have someone place a hand under the lower back; the body should press down on the hand until the lower back is curled forward.

NOTE: If the curl-up cannot be done as described, it is possible to decrease the resistance by placing the hands alongside the hips instead of over the chest. To increase the resistance, weights can be held on the chest while doing the exercise. Another method is to use an incline board and raise the board to provide a greater amount of resistance.

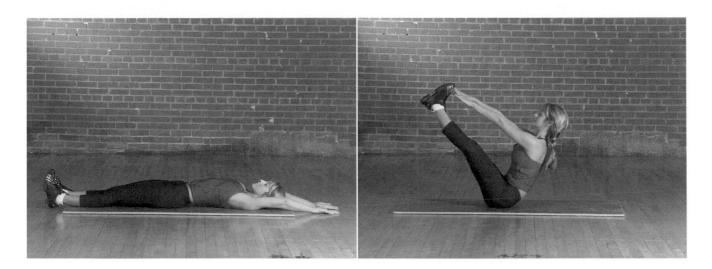

V-Sit

Starting Position: Lie flat on the floor with the legs straight and the arms fully extended above the head.

Action: Raise the legs and arms at the same time, and touch the hands and feet together above the body. Hold this position for one second and return to the starting position.

Precautions: Keep the arms and legs straight while doing the exercise. Do not jerk or make any unnecessary motion to assist in the movement.

Roman Chair Curl-Up

Starting Position: Lie flat on the floor with knees bent over a bench. The hands are folded over the chest. To increase resistance, weights can be held on the chest.

Action: Curl up and rotate the body until right side of body touches left knee and return to the starting position. On next repetition rotate body to the right knee.

Precautions: Do not arch back during the curl-up. Do not jerk the body during the movement.

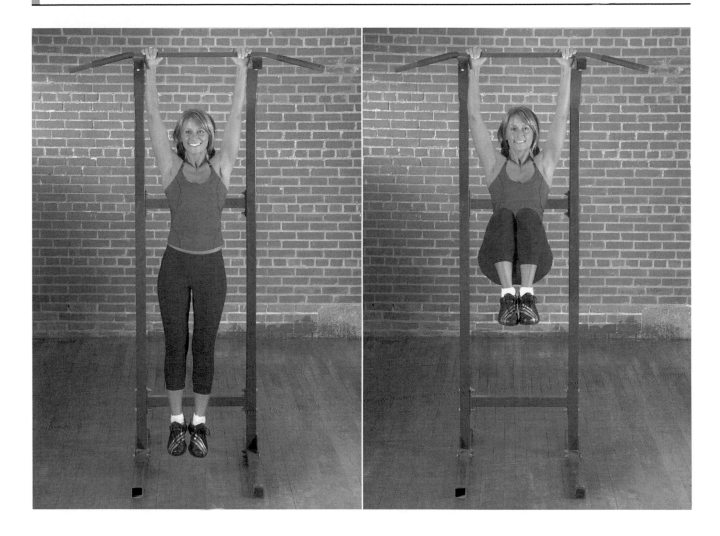

Hanging Knee-Up

Starting Position: Grasp the bar and allow the body to be completely extended.

Action: Raise the legs, knees bent, until the knees touch the chest, and return to the starting position.

Precautions: Raise the legs slowly without jerking to assist in the movement.

Sitting Knee-Up

Starting Position: Sit on the end of the bench with the legs extended away from the bench. Lean the upper torso back and grasp the bench with the hands.

Action: Slowly bend your knees and raise them to the chest. Touch the knees against the chest, and return to the starting position.

Precautions: Hold the feet and knees together during the exercise. Do not jerk the body during the movement.

Side Bend

Starting Position: Stand upright with a dumbbell held in one hand and the arms completely extended.

Action: Bend sideways as far as possible toward the side with the dumbbell and return to the starting position. When the desired number of repetitions have been completed, change the dumbbell to the other hand and repeat the exercise to the other side.

Precautions: Do not jerk the weight or use any unnecessary motion in the movement.

Twists

Starting Position: Take a straddle seated position on a bench with the back straight and the head looking forward. Place the bar behind the neck and across the shoulders.

Action: Keep the pelvic region locked and twist the upper torso as far as possible to the right. Return to the starting position, and then twist to the left and return to the starting position.

Precautions: Squeeze with the knees against the bench to keep the hips from rotating. Do not jerk the body during the movement.

MIDSECTION

Crunches

Starting Position: Lie flat on the floor and place your hands behind your head. Flex the hips and knees to a 90 degree angle.

Action: Life your shoulders off the floor, moving your head and elbows toward the knees, and then return to the starting position.

Precautions: Do not arch the back during the crunch. Do not jerk the body during the movement.

Note: This exercise especially stimulates the rectus abdominis. To exercise and place emphasis on the obliques, alternate placing the right elbow to the left knee and then place the left elbow to the right knee.

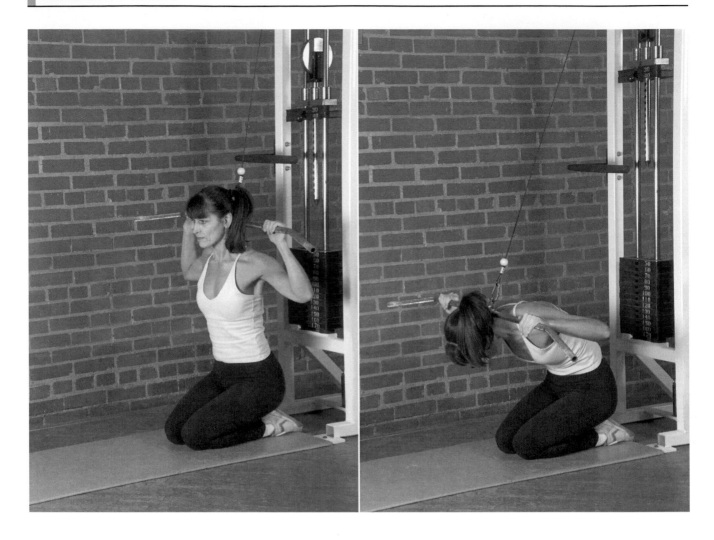

High Pulley Crunches

Starting Position: Kneel down and place the bar behind the neck.

Action: Curl the torso and move the chest toward the thighs and then return to the starting position.

Precautions: Do not use a heavy weight with this exercise. Focus on producing tension on the abdominals without using a jerking motion.

Machine Crunches

Starting Position: Sit in the machine and grasp the handles and hook the feet under the pads.

Action: Curl the chest toward the thighs and return to the starting position.

Precautions: Use a weight that can be moved smoothly without a jerking motion.

Incline Bench Sit-Up

Starting Position: Lie on the incline bench and hook the feet under the pads. Place the hands behind the neck.

Action: Move the torso upward by using a curling motion of the abdominal wall, and then return to the starting position.

Precautions: Do not jerk the body during the movement.

NOTE: This exercise can be done by twisting alternately to each side on successive repetitions. This will further stimulate the use of the obliques.

Roman Chair Side Bends

Starting Position: Place the hip on the support pad and hook the feet under the lower pads with the body just above horizontal. Place the hand behind the head.

Action: Lift and twist the body upward and then return to the starting position. Continue on the same side for a set and then change sides.

Precautions: Do not use a jerking movement and do not allow the body to go below the horizontal plane while doing the exercise.

Leg Splits

Starting Position: Lie flat on the left side of the body with the left hand and arm under the head. Use the right arm to support the body in the proper position during the exercise.

Action: Raise the right leg as high as possible and return to the starting position. When the desired number of repetitions have been completed on the left side, change to the right side and repeat the exercise.

Precautions: Keep the leg straight at all times, and do not jerk the body in the movement.

NOTE: To increase the resistance, weights can be added to the feet and ankles.

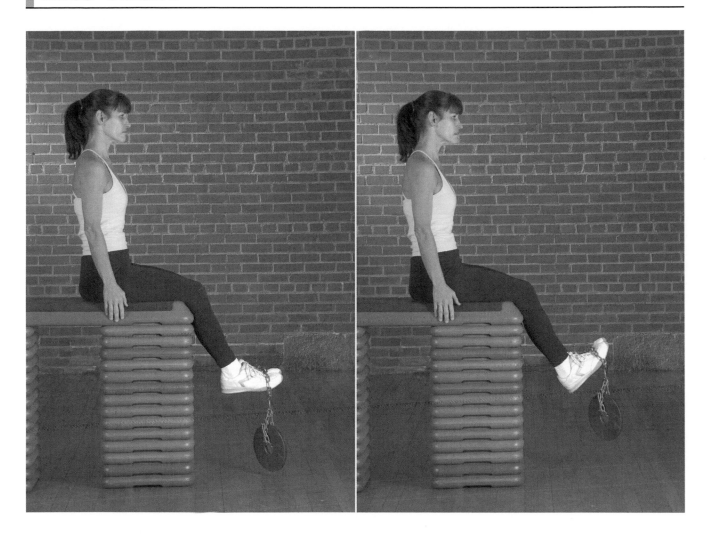

Toe Raise

Starting Position: Sit on the edge of a table with the lower legs hanging over the side. Grasp the side of the table with the hands to maintain balance. Attach a weight to the tocs of the foot with a chain, strap, or rope.

Action: Lift the toes upward toward the shins as far as possible. Return to the starting position.

Precautions: Isolate the movement of the front part of the foot, and do the exercise slowly.

NOTE: This exercise can also be performed using one foot at a time.

Front Leg Kick

Starting Position: Stand erect with the left leg attached to pulley from the machine. Maintain balance by holding on to a support. The left foot is approximately sixteen inches behind the right foot.

Action: Extend the left leg forward and as high as possible. Return to the starting position. When the repetitions for the left leg have been completed, switch to the right leg.

Precautions: Keep the leg straight at all times, and do not bend the knee. Do the exercise slowly to maintain balance.

Side Leg Kick

Starting Position: Stand erect and sideways to the machine with the right leg attached to the pulley. Maintain balance by holding on to a support. The right leg is crossed over the left leg away from the machine as far as possible.

Action: Extend the right leg outward as far as possible. Return to the starting position. When the repetitions for the right leg have been completed, switch to the left.

Precautions: Keep the leg straight at all times, and do not bend the knee. Do the exercise slowly to maintain balance.

Leg Press

Starting Position: Take a seat in the machine, and grasp the handles on both sides of the seat with the feet on the pedals. Keep the back straight.

Action: Push forward until the legs are fully extended. Return to the starting position.

Precautions: Do not use any unnecessary body motion to aid in the movement.

LEGS–FRONT

Vertical Leg Press

Starting Position: Lie flat on the back with the legs bent and the feet against the bar. The hips should be directly beneath the feet.

Action: Push the bar upward until the legs are fully extended. Return to the starting position.

Precautions: Since the resistance on this exercise has a tendency to cause the pressure in the chest cavity to increase, the lifter should keep the mouth open during the movement.

NOTE: This exercise can be modified so that the calf muscles can be trained by extending the front of the foot while the legs are extended.

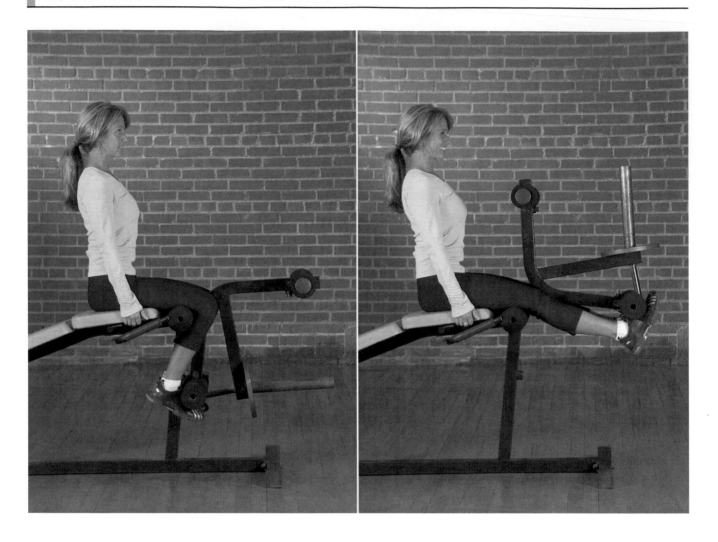

Leg Extension

Starting Position: Sit on the edge of the seat and place your feet behind the pads of the machine. Support the body by grasping the sides of the bench. Keep the back straight.

Action: Fully extend the legs to a locked position. Return to the starting position.

Precautions: Do not jerk the weight or use any unnecessary body motion in the movement.

NOTE: It is possible to isolate the leg muscles by doing single leg extensions.

Bench Jump

Starting Position: Stand erect with the body sideways to the bench.

Action: Flex the knees and jump sideways over the bench. Touch this side and return to the starting side.

Precautions: Use the arms to aid in the jump to increase height. Make sure to flex the ankles, knees, and hips when landing to reduce the downward shock.

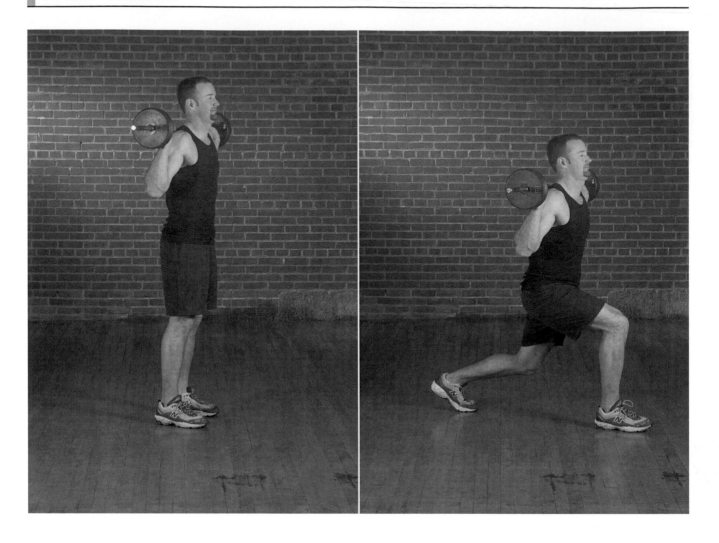

Lunge Squat

Starting Position: Stand erect with the feet about shoulder width apart. Place the bar behind the neck and across the shoulders. Keep the head up and the back straight.

Action: Step forward with the right leg and lower the body until the left knee is about twelve inches from the floor. Return to the starting position. Repeat the same action with the left leg, and return to the starting position.

Precautions: Keep the back straight and the head up during the movement. Do not bounce at the bottom part of the exercise.

NOTE: This exercise can also be accomplished by using dumbbells. Hold the dumbbells with the arms completely extended along the sides of the body and use the same action as contained in the above information.

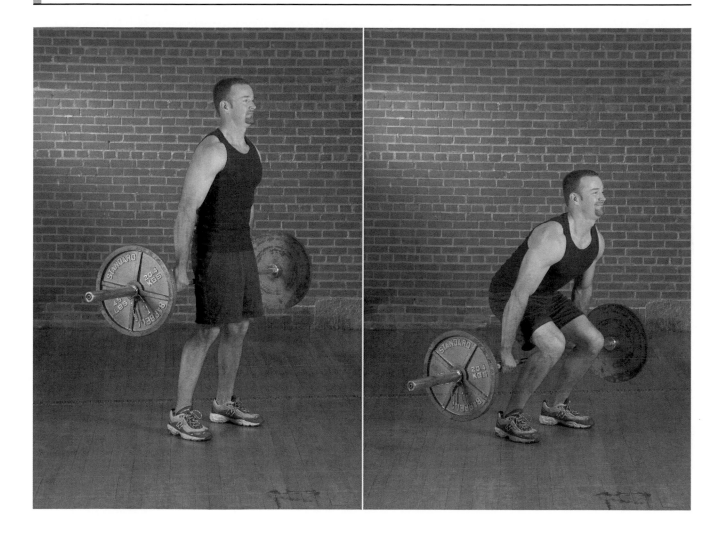

Hack Squat

Starting Position: Stand erect with the feet slightly wider than shoulder width. The bar is placed behind the back and against the thighs. Grasp the bar with an overhand grip, and keep the head up and the back straight.

Action: Lower the body until the thighs are parallel with the floor. Return to the starting position.

Precautions: Keep the upper torso straight to remove stress from the lower back. Do not bounce at the bottom of the squat.

NOTE: This exercise can be performed at any selected joint angle depending on the needs of the person training.

Trap Bar

The trap bar is an excellent lead-up exercise to squats. It is a safe exercise, as you do not need a spotter. You can also combine shoulder shrugs with this exercise.

Starting Position: Stand with the feet slightly wider than shoulder width. The toes are pointed slightly out. Lower the body by bending at the hips and extending the gluteal area. (Think of sitting in a chair.) Grasp the hand grips on the bar, which will allow the weight to be in perfect alignment with the body's center of gravity. Keep the head up.

Action: Spread the chest and lock the lower back, then extend the legs until you are in a standing position. Then return to the starting position.

Precautions: Keep the upper torso straight to remove stress from the lower back. Rounding the back can cause stress and injury.

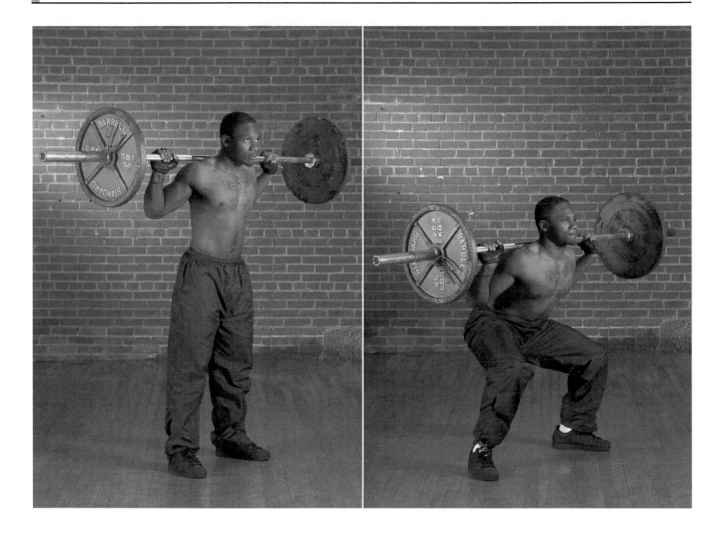

Back Squat

Starting Position: Stand erect with the feet slightly wider than shoulder width. The toes are pointed slightly out. Place the bar behind the neck and across the shoulders. Keep the head up and the back straight.

Action: Spread the chest and lock the lower back. The downward movement is started by bending at the hips and sticking out the gluteal area. (Think of sitting in a chair.) Lower the body until the thighs are parallel with the floor. Return to the starting position.

Precautions: Have partners assist as spotters during the exercise. Keep back straight and chest high throughout the movement. Rounding the back can place stress on spine and cause injury. Do not bounce at the bottom of the squat. As a safety device, place a bench behind the lifter, which will allow the lifter to sit down if balance is lost.

Note: This exercise can be performed to any selected joint angle of the legs depending on the needs of the person training.

Front Squat

Starting Position: Stand erect with the feet slightly wider than shoulder width. The toes are pointed slightly out. Hold the bar in front of the neck and across the front of the shoulders and upper chest. The position of the elbows and hands are important. The elbows should be in a high position with the upper arm parallel to the floor. The hands are open so that the weight is supported on the front of the shoulders and upper chest. Keep the head up and the back straight.

Action: The downward movement is started by bending at the hips and sticking out the gluteal area. (Think of sitting in a chair.) Lower the body until the thighs are parallel to the floor. Return to the starting position.

Precautions: Keep the upper torso straight to remove stress from the lower back. Do not bounce at the bottom of the squat.

NOTE: This exercise can be performed to any selected joint angle of the legs depending on the needs of the person training.

Hang Clean

Starting Position: Place the feet slightly wider than shoulder width. Grasp the bar with an overhand grip slightly wider than the shoulders and bend the knees and hips until the bar touches mid-thigh. Keep the head up and the arms fully extended.

Action: Straighten the legs to lift the weight. Keep the arms extended. Pull bar up in a straight path and keep the bar close to the body. Push forward with the hips as the legs extend upward. As the body starts to become erect, pull upward with the arms fully extended. As the bar reaches maximum height, drop the body under the bar by flexing the hips and knees into a squat position and catch the weight by moving the elbows under the bar and support the bar across the chest at the base of the neck. Stand up by extending the hips and knees to a fully erect position. To return to the starting position lower the bar in a controlled fashion by keeping the arms fully extended and squat with the legs until the weight touches the floor.

Precautions: Be sure you use an explosive movement in this exercise. Start with a light weight and practice the technique before using heavy weights.

Even though this exercise is placed in the leg section, it is a tremendous total body exercise and exercises many of the muscle groups in the entire body.

Power Clean

Starting Position: Place the feet slightly wider than shoulder width, and allow the shins to touch the bar. Bend down and grasp the bar with an overhand grip with the hands about shoulder width on the bar. Bend the knees until the hips are slightly higher than the knees. Keep the head up and the arms fully extended.

Action: Straighten the legs to lift the weight. Keep the arms extended. Pull bar up in a straight path and keep the bar close to the body. Push forward with the hips as the legs extend upward. As the body starts to become erect, pull upward with the arms fully extended. As the bar reaches maximum height, drop the body under the bar by flexing the hips and knees into a squat position and catch the weight by moving the elbows under the bar and support the bar across the chest at the base of the neck. Stand up by extending the hips and knees to a fully erect position. To return to the starting position lower the bar in a controlled fashion by keeping the arms fully extended and squat with the legs until the weight touches the floor.

Precautions: Be sure you use an explosive movement in this exercise. Start with a light weight and practice the technique before using heavy weights.

NOTE: This exercise can be performed to any selected joint angle of the legs depending on the needs of the person training.

Even though this exercise is placed in the leg section, it is a tremendous total body exercise and exercises many of the muscle groups in the entire body.

Standing Heel Raise

Starting Position: Stand erect with the feet about eight inches apart. Place the bar behind the neck and across the shoulders. Keep the head up and the back straight. Put the balls of the feet on a four-inch wooden board, and allow the heels to lower as far as possible.

Action: Raise the body as high as possible. Return to the starting position.

Precautions: Keep the body erect, and do the exercise slowly to maintain balance.

Single-Heel Raise

Starting Position: Place the right foot on a four-inch board, and allow the heel to lower as far as possible. Hold a dumbbell in the right hand with the arm extended. Keep the body erect and balanced by holding on to a support with the left hand.

Action: Raise the body as high as possible. Return to the starting position. When the repetitions for the right leg have been completed, switch to the left leg.

Precautions: Keep the body erect, and do the exercise slowly to maintain balance.

Sitting Heel Raise

Starting Position: Take a seated position on the bench. Place the bar across the top of the thigh and support the weight with the hands. Place the balls of the feet on a four-inch wooden board, and allow the heels to lower as far as possible.

Action: Raise the heels as high as possible. Return to the starting position.

Precautions: Keep the body erect, and do not bounce at the bottom of the movement.

Toe Extension

Starting Position: Take a seat in the machine, and fully extend the legs. Grasp the handles on both sides of the seat, and keep the back straight. Slide the feet off the pedals until only the balls of the feet make contact.

Action: Extend the toes as far forward as possible. Return to the starting position.

Precautions: Keep the legs straight, and do the exercise slowly.

NOTE: To change the calf development, it is possible to use different toe placements on the pedals as shown in the pictures.

Leg Curl

Starting Position: Lie face downward on the bench with the legs extended and the backs of the feet against the pads. Grasp the sides of the bench to maintain balance.

Action: Lift the feet upward until the pads areas close to the buttocks as possible. Return to the starting position.

Precautions: Movement should be entirely in the knee joint. Avoid unnecessary jerking or body movement.

Glute-Ham Raise

Starting Position: Take a prone position on the machine with the lower part of the body on the machine and the upper torso bent forward to form a 90° angle. The hands are interlocked behind the neck.

Action: Raise the upper torso upward until the body is parallel to the floor. Start to bend the knees and continue to raise the upper torso until it is also perpendicular to the floor. Hold this position for one count, and then return to the starting position.

Precautions: Do not jerk or use any unnecessary motion to assist in the movement. There should not be any undue stress on the lower back while doing this exercise.

Strength Training for Athletes

Anyone who wishes to improve athletic performance can do so by utilizing strength training. As indicated in chapter 1, to increase power, the rate of doing work, one must increase either strength or velocity or, if possible, both of these factors. Since all athletic contests are time related, a person who can increase work output for a given time frame will be more successful.

Research indicates a high correlation between strength levels and velocity. Strength training was once thought to reduce flexibility or cause a person to be muscle-bound and slow. The research refutes this myth and indicates instead that by using weight training through a full range of motion, athletes actually improve their flexibility and speed of movement.

The advantage of increased strength is important to both male and female athletes. Both can engage in a strength development program to increase their efficiency. At the end of this chapter, an athlete or coach can devise an individualized strength training program for any sport.

STRESS AND OVERTRAINING

Some years ago Hans Selye, a medical doctor, discovered that all stressors that the human body encounters produce very similar biochemical responses. He found that stressors cause the body to go through stages, which Selye termed the general adaptation syndrome (GAS). The stages are as follows:

1. Alarm reaction—This is the initial response to the stressor and causes a mobilization of the body systems to withstand the stressor. This upsets homeostasis, or the body's equilibrium. An example is the stress involved in starting a strength program.
2. Stage of resistance—During this stage the body improves its capacity and builds up reserves to combat the stressors. This stage represents the objective of a physical conditioning program. As a result of this stage in a strength training program, the body increases its ability to exert force and has a greater work output.
3. Stage of exhaustion (overtraining)—This stage is brought about by the body's inability to withstand chronic stress. It can result in exhaustion caused by overtraining; in the sport world, it is sometimes referred to as athletic staleness. Some of the symptoms of this stage are as follows:
   - increased resting heart rate
   - increased exercise heart rate
   - decreased appetite

- decreased body weight
- sleep loss
- decreased sex drive
- generalized body aches and pains
- increased release of catecholamines (hormones) from the adrenal gland
- decreased sports efficiency, loss of concentration, and errors in judgment
- interpersonal problems and conflicts
- illness and injury

When planning a training program, one must take into consideration the total stressor influence that is going to act upon the athlete. Such things as training loads, family influence, workload at school, social interactions, and employment are important. Always remember that too much stress leads to overtraining and the stage of exhaustion.

PERIODIZATION

To prevent overtraining and bring about peak performance in strength development, a system of training known as periodization has been recommended. Periodization is a training approach that involves dividing the training year into major phases or cycles, during which the stress of training is manipulated by varying the volume and intensity of the training stimulus during the selected phases. This combats overtraining and the onset of the stage of exhaustion (athletic staleness).

Volume is the amount of training completed in a given training or workout period. In strength training it represents all the sets and repetitions and can be quantified as the total number of pounds lifted. *Intensity* is the difficulty of the training stimulus. In strength training it is determined by the percentage of a one-repetition maximum (1 RM).

The periodization model for strength training (see Table 6.1) is divided into five yearly phases: hypertrophy, basic strength, strength and power, peaking or maintenance, and active rest.

Table 6.1	Periodization Model for Strength Training				
Phase	Hyper-trophy	Basic Strength	Strength and Power	Peaking or Maintenance*	Active Rest
Sets†	3–10	3–5	3–5	1–3	
Repetitions	8–12	4–6	2–3	1–3	
Days/Week	3–4	3–5	3–5	1–5	
Intensity cycle (weeks)‡	2–3/1	2–4/1	2–3/1	—	
Intensity	low	high	high	very high to low	
Volume	high	moderate to high	low	very low	

*Peaking for sports with a definite climax or maintenance for sports with a long season such as football.

†Does not include warmup sets.

‡Ratio of number of heavy training weeks to light training weeks.

Source: Adapted from Michael Stone and Harold O'Bryant, Weight Training: A Scientific Approach, (Edina, Minn.: Burgess International Group, 1987), 123.

Periodization Phases

Hypertrophy Phase: In this phase the goal is to stimulate the tissues that make up the joint-lever system and bring about an increase in the mass of the tissue. The focus is on increasing the size of the muscle cells; thus the term *hypertrophy* is used. During this phase the volume (number of exercises, sets, and repetitions) will be high, and the intensity (percentage of 1 RM) will be relatively low. This will cause the body to release chemical modulators to increase lean body mass. This was explained on page 33 of Chapter 3.

Basic Strength Phase: During this phase the intensity will be relatively high, and the volume will be moderate to high. The goal is to stimulate the increased lean body mass obtained in the hypertrophy phase and make it as strong as possible.

Strength and Power Phase: After completing the basic strength phase, the goal is to continue to increase strength, but also increase the power output. This phase focuses not only on stimulating the tissues that produce a force, but also on stimulating the systems that provide the energy to allow the body to move very rapidly. In many sports the first three steps are the most critical in achieving success. During this phase the intensity is high and the volume is low.

Peaking or Maintenance Phase: This is the phase when the athlete is competing and more time must be used to increase skill and prepare for games. Maintaining the strength training effects is important, and thus a strength training program is a critical part of this phase. During this time the volume is low and, depending on the day of the week, the intensity may be either very high or very low.

Active Rest: This phase follows completion of the competition phase and refers to participating in some other activity or the same activity at very low volumes and intensities. The length of active rest depends on the sport and the athlete's needs. This phase allows the athlete to combat overtraining, which leads to decreased performance.

Intensity Cycle: During each phase there is an intensity cycle which is a ratio of the number of heavy training weeks to light training weeks. For example, if an athlete was in the hypertrophy phase, they would engage in 2–3 weeks of relatively heavy resistance followed by one week of light resistance. This allows the cells of the body to accommodate to the training stimulus and bring about the physiological changes desired in each conditioning phase.

In order to determine the resistance for any given phase, you use the following table:

Guidelines to Determine Percentage of a One–Repetition Maximum (1RM)	
Repetitions	**% of 1RM (Range)**
1	100
2	90–95+
3	87.5–95
5	75–87.5
10	60–80

For example, if you were in the hypertrophy phase, using 10 repetitions in the heavy cycle, you might select 80% 1RM and then, in the light cycle, you might reduce the resistance as low as 60% 1RM for 10 repetitions.

Factors in Setting Up a Periodization Plan

When setting up a periodization plan, the following factors should be considered:

1. What are the demands of the sport? How can these best be developed? What is the athlete trying to develop at this time of the training year? What facilities are available for training? How much time is available for training?
2. What are the demands of the position? Is it a wide receiver, a power forward, or a center-blocker in volleyball?
3. Determine the athlete's strengths and weaknesses. What is the basic training background of the athlete? Should the athlete engage in a beginning strength program to develop overall strength before starting a periodized training plan?

In addition to considering the previous factors in writing strength training programs for athletes, one must also understand the concept of using core and supplementary exercises to bring about the desired changes to increase performance.

Table 6.2 — Strength Training Exercises for Specific Sports

	Arm curl	Back raise	Bench flys	Bench jump	Bench press	Bent-arm pullover	Bent-over lateral raise	Bent-over rowing	Mid-section	Dead lift	Dip	Dumbbell bent-over rowing	Dumbbell curl	Glute-Ham Raise	Heel raise	
Archery	X		X				X	X	X				X	X		
Badminton			X		X	X			X					X		
Baseball					X				X		X		X	X	X	
Basketball	X			X	X				X				X	X		
Bicycling									X						X	
Bowling	X	X							X					X		
Boxing	X		X		X				X		X		X			
Canoeing	X				X	X	X	X	X							
Climbing	X				X			X	X			X		X		
Crew	X	X			X	X		X	X			X	X	X		
Diving					X				X					X		
Fencing					X				X			X		X		

CORE AND SUPPLEMENTARY EXERCISES

A core exercise is a strength exercise that uses a large muscle mass and is usually a multiple-joint exercise. Examples of core exercises are the bench press, incline press, squats, leg press, and power clean. Core exercises form the foundation of the strength training program and contribute to total body strength.

Supplementary exercises utilize a smaller muscle mass. Many times they are single-joint exercises that increase the strength of the specific muscles used in a given activity.

When training the athlete should always do the core exercises before doing the supplementary exercises.

Table 6.2 contains a list of various sports and strength training exercises that could be considered to increase the strength of the muscles used in the sport. An athlete can now select one or more exercises for each specific body part.

	Incline bench press	Lat pull-down	Leg curl	Leg extension	Leg press	Neck exercise	Overhead press	Power clean–Hang clean	Sitting heel raise	Seated rowing	Side lateral raise	Single-heel raise	Squat	Toe extension	Trap Bar	Triceps extension	Upright rowing	Wrist curl

Continued.

Table 6.2 | Strength Training Exercises for Specific Sports–Continued

	Arm curl	Back raise	Bench flys	Bench jump	Bench press	Bent-arm pullover	Bent-over lateral raise	Bent-over rowing	Mid-section	Dead lift	Dip	Dumbbell bent-over rowing	Dumbbell curl	Glute-Ham Raise	Heel raise
Field hockey	X	X	X		X				X					X	X
Football	X				X	X			X	X	X		X	X	X
Golf	X						X		X						
Handball		X			X				X						
Hockey	X				X		X		X		X			X	X
Martial arts	X	X			X		X		X					X	X
Racquetball		X			X		X		X		X				
Rugby	X				X				X	X	X		X	X	X
Skating									X					X	
Skiing	X				X				X					X	X
Soccer					X	X			X					X	
Softball	X		X		X		X		X			X	X	X	X
Squash	X	X			X				X	X		X	X	X	
Swimming		X			X	X		X	X	X				X	
Tennis	X	X	X		X				X					X	X
Track—distance		X			X			X	X	X				X	
Track—sprints	X	X							X	X				X	
Field events	X	X	X		X	X			X					X	
Volleyball		X			X	X								X	X
Water Polo	X	X			X	X			X			X		X	X
Wrestling	X				X				X		X			X	

	Incline bench press	Lat pull-down	Leg curl	Leg extension	Leg press	Neck exercise	Overhead press	Power clean-Hang clean	Sitting heel raise	Seated rowing	Side lateral raise	Single-heel raise	Squat	Toe extension	Trap Bar	Triceps extension	Upright rowing	Wrist curl

OFF–SEASON STRENGTH TRAINING PROGRAM

Here is an example of how the information in tables 6.1 and 6.2 can be used to write an off-season strength program for a football defensive lineman who is in the hypertrophy phase of the training year. Using this program will increase the amount of lean body mass (hypertrophy) and also increase strength.

Sport: Football

Position: Defensive Lineman

Phase: Hypertrophy

Intensity Cycle: ☒ Heavy / ☐ Light / ☐ # of Weeks ___3___

Core Exercises: Bench press, Back squat, Power Clean

Supplementary Exercises: Partner resistance for neck, Arm curl, Dumbbell triceps extension, Upright rowing, Lat pull-down, Roman chair curl-up, Glute-ham raise

You can use the Sports Training Worksheet in Appendix E to write the program. On page 152 is an example of this strength training program.

Modified Periodization Program

Many athletes, especially at the high school level, participate in more than one sport and cannot follow a full year of periodized training such as that of a single-sport athlete. Some athletes may play football, then basketball, and then baseball. They still want to obtain the benefits of a good strength program so that they can continue to increase their power output and obtain optimal performance levels.

Using a modified periodization program has been highly successful in bringing about beneficial results. This program is a combination of core and supplementary exercises. The core exercises have both a five-set day and a three-set day for each exercise.

Five-Set Day-Heavy Intensity

1. Warm-up
2. Three sets at 80 percent of a 1 RM for four repetitions
3. Two sets at 90 percent of a 1 RM for two repetitions

Three-Set Day-Light Intensity

1. Warm-up
2. Two sets at 80 percent of a 1 RM for four repetitions
3. One set at 90 percent of a 1 RM for two repetitions

Supplementary Exercises: Generally do two sets of 10 RM. In the off-season usually do no more than five different exercises, and in-season usually do two or three different exercises.

The act of periodization in the off-season comes into effect as the athlete is manipulating the training days from heavy to light and also manipulating the training weeks from heavy to light throughout the entire off-season.

During the playing seasons you could strength train two days a week with the 5-set (heavy) day on either Monday or Tuesday and the 3-set (light) day on Wednesday or Thursday. The athlete will still be obtaining a strength stimulus and have time to recover before game day. The author has conducted research with multi-sport athletes and found that significant strength gains can be made in both the off-season and the playing season.

On page 153 is an example of an off-season program for a three sport athlete.

Heavy			Light			Heavy		
Week 1			Week 2			Week 3		
M	W	F	M	W	F	M	W	F
5 sets Heavy	3 sets Light	5 sets Heavy	3 sets Light	5 sets Heavy	3 sets Light	5 sets Heavy	3 sets Light	5 sets Heavy

NEBRASKA ATHLETIC TEST

The major reason an athlete engages in a strength training program is to increase power output. As stated earlier, power output determines how much work can be accomplished in a given amount of time.

The University of Nebraska has one of the most outstanding programs in the world to condition athletes. The program uses four tests that seem to predict athletic performance. These tests can be utilized to determine if the strength training program is making positive changes that will aid the athlete. The four tests are the ten-yard dash, the forty-yard dash, the twenty-yard shuttle run, and the vertical jump.

All that is needed to administer the tests are a stopwatch, a wall with a measuring board marked in one-half-inch increments, and a gym floor or grassy area. A worksheet for this test can be found in Appendix G.

THE SPORT EXPERIENCE

Write an individualized strength training program for your selected sport and record your work on the sports training worksheet in Appendix E or the modified periodization worksheet in Appendix F. In addition, take the Nebraska Athletic Test as explained on the worksheet in Appendix G to determine how well you perform before starting your strength program.

Sports Training Worksheet

Name: _John Jones_

Sport: _Football_   Position: _Defensive Lineman_

Phase: _Hypertrophy_   Intensity Cycle: [X] Heavy / [ ] Light / [ ] # of Weeks _3_

Core Exercises

Upper Body: _Bench Press_

Lower Body: _Back Squat_   Sets _4_ / Reps _10_ / Recovery _3 mins_

Total Body: _Power Clean_   Resistance _80_ % 1RM

Supplementary Exercises

Body Part	Exercise
Neck	Partner resistance
Arms	
Biceps	Arm curl
Triceps	Dumbbell triceps extension
Shoulders	Upright rowing
Back	Lat pull-down
Midsection	Roman chair curl-up (30 reps with body weight)
Legs-Back	Elute-ham raise

Sets _3_ / Reps _10_ / Recovery _2 mins_

Resistance _80_ % 1RM

Modified Periodization Program

Name: _Alice Smith_

Sports: _Volleyball, Basketball, Track_

Positions: _Middle Blocker, Center, High Jump_

In-Season: Off-Season [x]

Core Exercises

Five-set Day: 3 sets 3 4 reps at 80% 1 RM
2 sets 3 2 reps at 90% 1 RM

Three-set Day: 2 sets 3 4 reps at 80% 1 RM
1 set 3 2 reps at 90% 1 RM

Recovery Time: _3 mins_

Exercise	1 RM	80% 1 RM	90% 1 RM
Bench Press	150	120	135
Front Squat	200	160	180
Powerclean	150	120	135

Supplementary Exercises

Exercise	Sets	Reps	Recovery	Resistance
Glute-Ham raise	2	10 RM	2 mins	30
Crunches	2	30	2 mins	Body weight
Triceps press down	2	10 RM	2 mins	65
Lat pulldown	2	10 RM	2 mins	100

7 Bodybuilding and Physique Training

Bodybuilder is defined as a person who uses strength training to obtain a more muscular physique. This broad definition includes nearly all people who lift weights. As indicated earlier, the majority of men and women who enroll in beginning weight training classes desire to "look better"; in other words, they wish to be "bodybuilders."

In a body building program, the desired outcome is an increase in lean body mass (hypertrophy), especially of the muscle cells. In order to obtain this objective the volume (sets and reps) for each body part must be increased. This will cause the body to release chemical modulators that bring about the desired increase in lean body mass. This concept is further explained on page 33 of chapter 3.

The training programs described previously can help develop the different muscles of the body and bring about a more muscular physique.

PHYSIQUE ATHLETES

Another group of individuals who have a great desire to affect the muscular system of the body are classified as physique athletes. The elite athletes in this group earn Mr. America, Mr. Universe, and Mr. Olympia titles. This group also includes females who compete for similar titles such as Miss America and Miss Universe.

Most physique contests are judged according to the following criteria:

1. *Symmetry:* the overall balance of development of the various body parts and muscle groups
2. *Muscularity:* how well a muscle is developed in regard to size, definition, and hardness
3. *Presentation:* personal grooming, posing ability, and how individuals project themselves

Even when using a mirror, it is impossible for people to see themselves as they really are. Many times we view ourselves quite differently from what is reflected. To record changes and understand more about your body, you should measure the various body parts at the start of a training program and take periodic measurements to determine how the training is affecting the body size.

Another assessment method is to have a series of photographs taken of yourself in a swimsuit. Take photos of the front, side, and back, first with the body in a relaxed position and then with the muscles flexed. This information can be used later, after you have been training, to determine the changes that have taken place.

To a great extent, a person's body type is determined before birth, but through proper training, an individual can build some areas and reduce others. The purpose of this chapter is to explain various types of physique training programs one might engage in to bring about those body changes.

No one system of training is best because each individual is different. Experiment with different systems of training and find the method that works best. A combination of systems may bring about the desired results and stimulate the body to make rapid gains. Keep accurate records of how the body responds to the different methods of training. Comparing the progress made, makes it easier to select the most beneficial training regimen.

SYSTEMS OF TRAINING

Set System

The set system is the most popular type of training to develop strength. In this system the person does an exercise for a given number of repetitions, or a set, then rests before performing another set. A variation of this system is referred to as *supersets*, in which an exercise set for a particular muscle group is followed immediately by an exercise set for the antagonist muscle. For example, a person could do a set of arm curls for the biceps and then do a set of triceps extensions for the triceps. This combination would be one superset.

Another variation of this type of training is known as the super multiple set system. In this training system the lifter completes all of the sets for a given muscle group and then follows this exercise with the same number of sets for the antagonist muscle group.

Bodybuilding programs increase the volume of the workout by using more than one exercise for a given body part. They also utilize multiple sets and eight or more repetitions per set. As explained in chapter 3, increasing the volume provides the stimuli that is thought to bring about the metabolic changes that cause hypertrophy (an increase in muscle cell size).

Split Routine

In bodybuilding the idea is to exercise every major muscle group in the body. This requires a great amount of time and work. To obtain the maximum development, the major body parts are split into groups, and the lifter works out six days a week but exercises the selected body parts on alternate days. For example, the arms, legs, and midsection might be exercised on Monday, Wednesday, and Friday, and the chest, shoulders, and back would be exercised on Tuesday, Thursday, and Saturday. This system is one of the most popular types of training that bodybuilders use. Often this training program incorporates supersets.

A variation of the split-routine system is known as the *blitz method*. This method is often utilized when the bodybuilder is preparing for a contest and wishes to obtain the maximum size and muscle definition, which is so important in competition. In this system a person might perform all the arm exercises one day, all the chest exercises the next day, the legs on the next day, and so on. This is a very strenuous and tiring method of training and is usually recommended for only a few weeks at a time.

Burns

Some bodybuilders include sets of rapid half-contractions, or "burns," in their workout. These sets produce a burning sensation in the muscle, which is thought to be caused by blood being forced into the muscle area to produce the so-called *muscle pump*. The lifter is trying to achieve a greater increase in the size of the musculature.

Forced Reps

In the forced reps method of training, a partner assists the lifter so that more repetitions with greater resistance can be accomplished. The partner can push the individual far beyond the normal point of fatigue, the hoped-for result being more strength and muscle-building stimulation. For example, an individual might do ten repetitions on the lat pull-down without assistance. When the person reaches the normal point of fatigue on the tenth repetition, the partner would assist the lifter through the sticking point for three to five more forced reps.

Preexhaustion

Most exercises in strength training are accomplished by a large muscle group working in conjunction with a smaller muscle group. For example, the back muscles work with the biceps of the arm in pull-ups. The small muscle may fatigue before the large muscle group, and as a result, the large muscle group does not receive the optimum resistance to bring about physiological changes, such as an increase in size.

The preexhaustion system is based on the idea of doing a preliminary isolation exercise to overload the large muscle group before doing the exercise that uses both the large and small muscle groups together. This technique theoretically would then fatigue the stronger group to make it weaker than the smaller muscle group, thus enabling the lifter to push the basic combination exercise to a point where both muscle groups would develop.

Pyramid System

This type of training consists of adding weight until the lifter can complete only one repetition. For example, a person may start doing the bench press with a set of 10 RM, then add enough weight to do 9 RM, then 8 RM, and so on until the final set would consist of 1 RM.

In the first type of pyramid the lifter went from light to heavy resistance. In another pyramid system the lifter goes from heavy to light resistance. After a warm-up set the lifter does a set of 1 to 2 RM, removes, for example, five pounds, and does the maximum number of repetitions, continuing in this way until only the weight of the bar or a small resistance remains.

The following section is a training program utilized by a student who placed first in the Mr. Collegiate USA contest.

MR. COLLEGIATE USA TRAINING PROGRAM

Basic Concepts

1. Every major muscle group in the body is exercised.
2. The musculature is worked as thoroughly as possible (achieving a "pumped" feeling).
3. Every set is preceded by a rest period of no more than ninety seconds.
4. Every repetition is performed in the strictest form.
5. The emphasis in bodybuilding is placed on doing the exercise movement correctly rather than trying to lift as much weight as possible.
6. A set of high repetitions begins each initial exercise per major muscle group, and as the resistance increases, the repetitions decrease.

Split Routine Program

Note: This program is to be followed six days a week. Exercise the midsection every day using a recovery time of two minutes.

First Day

Body Part	Exercise	
Midsection	Roman chair curl-up	3 sets of 75 reps, 3 sets of 80 reps
	V-sit	6 sets of 45 reps
	Hanging knee-up	6 sets of 25 reps
Biceps	Arm curl	1 set of 10 reps, 1 set of 8 reps, 3 sets of 6 reps
	Standing dumbbell curl	5 sets of 8 reps
	Incline dumbbell curl	5 sets of 8 reps
Triceps	Triceps press-down	4 sets of 8 reps, 1 set of 6 reps
	Lying barbell triceps extension	1 set of 20 reps, 4 sets of 8 reps
	Seated dumbbell triceps extension	2 sets of 10 reps, 2 sets of 8 reps, 1 set of 6 reps
Legs	Front squat	1 set of 20 reps, 1 set of 16 reps, 1 set of 12 reps, 1 set of 10 reps
	Lunge squat	1 set of 12 reps, 3 sets of 10 reps
	Leg curl	4 sets of 12 reps, 1 set of 20 reps
	Toe extension	5 sets of 20 reps, 3 sets of 25 reps
	Single-heel raise	6 sets of 8 reps

Second Day

Body Part	Exercise	
Midsection	Roman chair curl-up	3 sets of 75 reps, 3 sets of 80 reps
	V-sit	6 sets of 45 reps
	Hanging knee-up	6 sets of 25 reps
Chest	Dumbbell bench press	1 set of 10 reps, 3 sets of 8 reps, 1 set of 6 reps
	Bench press to neck	1 set of 12 reps, 1 set of 10 reps, 2 sets of 8 reps, 1 set of 6 reps
	Decline press	1 set of 10 reps, 1 set of 8 reps, 2 sets of 6 reps
	Bench flys	2 sets of 10 reps, 1 set of 8 reps, 2 sets of 6 reps
Back	Close grip lat pull-down	2 sets of 10 reps, 2 sets of 9 reps
	Regular grip lat pull-down	1 set of 10 reps, 2 sets of 8 reps, 1 set of 7 reps
	Seated rowing	3 sets of 10 reps, 1 set of 9 reps
Shoulders	Seated behind-neck press	2 sets of 7 reps, 2 sets of 6 reps, 5 sets of 12 reps
	Seated dumbbell press	5 sets of 12 reps
	Upright rowing	1 set of 10 reps, 4 sets of 9 reps
	Side lateral raise	5 sets of 8 reps

THE SPORT EXPERIENCE

Write a bodybuilding training program for yourself using the bodybuilding worksheet in Appendix H. Keep the following guidelines in mind:

1. Before starting your bodybuilding program, take all of your body measurements using the body measurement chart in Appendix A so you can plot your progress as you train.
2. If possible, take some photographs of yourself before starting your training program to compare how you look at various stages of your training program.
3. Work every major muscle group in your body.
4. Experiment with various bodybuilding systems of training during your program to determine which works best for you.

Appendix A

Body Measurement Chart

Name _____ Age _____

Date											
Body Weight											
Neck											
Shoulders											
Chest — Relaxed											
Chest — Flexed											
Upper Arm											
Relaxed — Right											
Relaxed — Left											
Flexed — Right											
Flexed — Left											
Forearm											
Relaxed — Right											
Relaxed — Left											
Flexed — Right											
Flexed — Left											
Waist											
Hips											
Thigh											
Relaxed — Right											
Relaxed — Left											
Flexed — Right											
Flexed — Left											
Calf											
Relaxed — Right											
Relaxed — Left											
Flexed — Right											
Flexed — Left											
Other Body Parts											

Appendix A

Body Measurement Chart

Name _____ Age _____

Date											
Body Weight											
Neck											
Shoulders											
Chest — Relaxed											
Chest — Flexed											
Upper Arm											
Relaxed — Right											
Relaxed — Left											
Flexed — Right											
Flexed — Left											
Forearm											
Relaxed — Right											
Relaxed — Left											
Flexed — Right											
Flexed — Left											
Waist											
Hips											
Thigh											
Relaxed — Right											
Relaxed — Left											
Flexed — Right											
Flexed — Left											
Calf											
Relaxed — Right											
Relaxed — Left											
Flexed — Right											
Flexed — Left											
Other Body Parts											

Appendix B

Strength Test

Name _____

PROCEDURES FOR ADMINISTERING STRENGTH TEST
1. Familiarize yourself with the six exercises utilized for the test.
   a. Lat Pull-down (LPD)—Start in a seated position and have someone hold the subject down at the shoulders. (page 99)
   b. Leg Extension (LE) (page 126)
   c. Bench Press (BP) (page 90)
   d. Curl-Up (CU)—Hold the weight on the front of the forehead, keep the knees flexed at a 100° angle, and have someone hold the feet. Curl forward and touch the elbows to the knees. (page 108)
   e. Leg Curl (LC)—flex the knee until the subject reaches a 90° angle. (page 141)
   f. Arm Curl (AC) (page 63)
2. Determine subject's weight in pounds.
3. Determine the amount of resistance to be used for each exercise. To obtain this number, multiply the body weight by the percentage of body weight given for each exercise in the chart at the bottom of the worksheet. Round the number to the lowest five pounds. For example, 54 is rounded to 50.
4. Record your resistance in the bottom of the worksheet.
5. Perform the maximum continuous number of repetitions for each exercise.
6. Determine the percentile rank for each exercise.

Strength Test													
Men							**Women**						
% Rank	**LPD**	**LE**	**BP**	**CU**	**LC**	**AC**	**% Rank**	**LPD**	**LE**	**BP**	**CU**	**LC**	**AC**
90	19	19	19	23	19	19	90	21	18	20	22	12	20
80	16	15	16	17	15	15	80	16	13	16	14	10	16
70	13	14	13	14	13	12	70	13	11	13	11	9	14
60	11	13	11	12	11	10	60	11	10	11	6	7	12
50	10	12	10	10	10	9	50	10	9	10	5	6	10
40	9	10	7	8	8	8	40	9	8	5	4	5	8
30	7	9	5	5	6	7	30	7	7	3	2	4	7
20	6	7	3	3	4	5	20	6	5	1	1	3	6
10	4	5	1	2	3	3	10	3	3	0	0	1	3
5	3	3	0	1	1	2	5	2	1	0	0	0	2

Adapted from the test developed by W. W. K. Hoeger and D. R. Hopkins and used with their permission.

7. Determine the strength category and number of points for each exercise.

% Rank	90	80–89	60–79	40–59	20–39	10–19	less than 10
Strength Category	Superior	Excellent	Good	Average	Fair	Poor	Very Poor
Points	19	17	15	13	11	9	7

8. Record percentile rank, strength category, and number of points below.

| Exercise | % Body Weight | | Resistance | Reps | % Rank | Strength Category | Pts |
	Men	Women					
1. Lat Pull-Down	.70	.45					
2. Leg Extension	.65	.50					
3. Bench Press	.75	.45					
4. Curl-Up	.16	.10					
5. Leg Curl	.32	.25					
6. Arm Curl	.35	.18					
						Total Points	

Appendix B
Strength Test

Name _____

PROCEDURES FOR ADMINISTERING STRENGTH TEST
1. Familiarize yourself with the six exercises utilized for the test.
    a. Lat Pull-down (LPD)—Start in a seated position and have someone hold the subject down at the shoulders. (page 99)
    b. Leg Extension (LE) (page 126)
    c. Bench Press (BP) (page 90)
    d. Curl-Up (CU)—Hold the weight on the front of the forehead, keep the knees flexed at a 100° angle, and have someone hold the feet. Curl forward and touch the elbows to the knees. (page 108)
    e. Leg Curl (LC)—flex the knee until the subject reaches a 90° angle. (page 141)
    f. Arm Curl (AC) (page 63)
2. Determine subject's weight in pounds.
3. Determine the amount of resistance to be used for each exercise. To obtain this number, multiply the body weight by the percentage of body weight given for each exercise in the chart at the bottom of the worksheet. Round the number to the lowest five pounds. For example, 54 is rounded to 50.
4. Record your resistance in the bottom of the worksheet.
5. Perform the maximum continuous number of repetitions for each exercise.
6. Determine the percentile rank for each exercise.

Strength Test													
Men							**Women**						
% Rank	**LPD**	**LE**	**BP**	**CU**	**LC**	**AC**	**% Rank**	**LPD**	**LE**	**BP**	**CU**	**LC**	**AC**
90	19	19	19	23	19	19	90	21	18	20	22	12	20
80	16	15	16	17	15	15	80	16	13	16	14	10	16
70	13	14	13	14	13	12	70	13	11	13	11	9	14
60	11	13	11	12	11	10	60	11	10	11	6	7	12
50	10	12	10	10	10	9	50	10	9	10	5	6	10
40	9	10	7	8	8	8	40	9	8	5	4	5	8
30	7	9	5	5	6	7	30	7	7	3	2	4	7
20	6	7	3	3	4	5	20	6	5	1	1	3	6
10	4	5	1	2	3	3	10	3	3	0	0	1	3
5	3	3	0	1	1	2	5	2	1	0	0	0	2

Adapted from the test developed by W. W. K. Hoeger and D. R. Hopkins and used with their permission.

7. Determine the strength category and number of points for each exercise.

% Rank	90	80–89	60–79	40–59	20–39	10–19	less than 10
Strength Category	Superior	Excellent	Good	Average	Fair	Poor	Very Poor
Points	19	17	15	13	11	9	7

8. Record percentile rank, strength category, and number of points below.

Exercise	% Body Weight		Resistance	Reps	% Rank	Strength Category	Pts
	Men	**Women**					
1. Lat Pull-Down	.70	.45					
2. Leg Extension	.65	.50					
3. Bench Press	.75	.45					
4. Curl-Up	.16	.10					
5. Leg Curl	.32	.25					
6. Arm Curl	.35	.18					
						Total Points	

Appendix B

Strength Test

Name _____

PROCEDURES FOR ADMINISTERING STRENGTH TEST
1. Familiarize yourself with the six exercises utilized for the test.
   a. Lat Pull-down (LPD)—Start in a seated position and have someone hold the subject down at the shoulders. (page 99)
   b. Leg Extension (LE) (page 126)
   c. Bench Press (BP) (page 90)
   d. Curl-Up (CU)—Hold the weight on the front of the forehead, keep the knees flexed at a 100° angle, and have someone hold the feet. Curl forward and touch the elbows to the knees. (page 108)
   e. Leg Curl (LC)—flex the knee until the subject reaches a 90° angle. (page 141)
   f. Arm Curl (AC) (page 63)
2. Determine subject's weight in pounds.
3. Determine the amount of resistance to be used for each exercise. To obtain this number, multiply the body weight by the percentage of body weight given for each exercise in the chart at the bottom of the worksheet. Round the number to the lowest five pounds. For example, 54 is rounded to 50.
4. Record your resistance in the bottom of the worksheet.
5. Perform the maximum continuous number of repetitions for each exercise.
6. Determine the percentile rank for each exercise.

Strength Test													
Men							**Women**						
% Rank	**LPD**	**LE**	**BP**	**CU**	**LC**	**AC**	**% Rank**	**LPD**	**LE**	**BP**	**CU**	**LC**	**AC**
90	19	19	19	23	19	19	90	21	18	20	22	12	20
80	16	15	16	17	15	15	80	16	13	16	14	10	16
70	13	14	13	14	13	12	70	13	11	13	11	9	14
60	11	13	11	12	11	10	60	11	10	11	6	7	12
50	10	12	10	10	10	9	50	10	9	10	5	6	10
40	9	10	7	8	8	8	40	9	8	5	4	5	8
30	7	9	5	5	6	7	30	7	7	3	2	4	7
20	6	7	3	3	4	5	20	6	5	1	1	3	6
10	4	5	1	2	3	3	10	3	3	0	0	1	3
5	3	3	0	1	1	2	5	2	1	0	0	0	2

Adapted from the test developed by W. W. K. Hoeger and D. R. Hopkins and used with their permission.

7. Determine the strength category and number of points for each exercise.

% Rank	90	80–89	60–79	40–59	20–39	10–19	less than 10
Strength Category	Superior	Excellent	Good	Average	Fair	Poor	Very Poor
Points	19	17	15	13	11	9	7

8. Record percentile rank, strength category, and number of points below.

Exercise	% Body Weight		Resistance	Reps	% Rank	Strength Category	Pts
	Men	**Women**					
1. Lat Pull-Down	.70	.45					
2. Leg Extension	.65	.50					
3. Bench Press	.75	.45					
4. Curl-Up	.16	.10					
5. Leg Curl	.32	.25					
6. Arm Curl	.35	.18					
						Total Points	

Appendix B

Strength Test

Name _____

PROCEDURES FOR ADMINISTERING STRENGTH TEST
1. Familiarize yourself with the six exercises utilized for the test.
   a. Lat Pull-down (LPD)—Start in a seated position and have someone hold the subject down at the shoulders. (page 99)
   b. Leg Extension (LE) (page 126)
   c. Bench Press (BP) (page 90)
   d. Curl-Up (CU)—Hold the weight on the front of the forehead, keep the knees flexed at a 100° angle, and have someone hold the feet. Curl forward and touch the elbows to the knees. (page 108)
   e. Leg Curl (LC)—flex the knee until the subject reaches a 90° angle. (page 141)
   f. Arm Curl (AC) (page 63)
2. Determine subject's weight in pounds.
3. Determine the amount of resistance to be used for each exercise. To obtain this number, multiply the body weight by the percentage of body weight given for each exercise in the chart at the bottom of the worksheet. Round the number to the lowest five pounds. For example, 54 is rounded to 50.
4. Record your resistance in the bottom of the worksheet.
5. Perform the maximum continuous number of repetitions for each exercise.
6. Determine the percentile rank for each exercise.

Strength Test													
Men							**Women**						
% Rank	**LPD**	**LE**	**BP**	**CU**	**LC**	**AC**	**% Rank**	**LPD**	**LE**	**BP**	**CU**	**LC**	**AC**
90	19	19	19	23	19	19	90	21	18	20	22	12	20
80	16	15	16	17	15	15	80	16	13	16	14	10	16
70	13	14	13	14	13	12	70	13	11	13	11	9	14
60	11	13	11	12	11	10	60	11	10	11	6	7	12
50	10	12	10	10	10	9	50	10	9	10	5	6	10
40	9	10	7	8	8	8	40	9	8	5	4	5	8
30	7	9	5	5	6	7	30	7	7	3	2	4	7
20	6	7	3	3	4	5	20	6	5	1	1	3	6
10	4	5	1	2	3	3	10	3	3	0	0	1	3
5	3	3	0	1	1	2	5	2	1	0	0	0	2

Adapted from the test developed by W. W. K. Hoeger and D. R. Hopkins and used with their permission.

7. Determine the strength category and number of points for each exercise.

% Rank	90	80–89	60–79	40–59	20–39	10–19	less than 10
Strength Category	Superior	Excellent	Good	Average	Fair	Poor	Very Poor
Points	19	17	15	13	11	9	7

8. Record percentile rank, strength category, and number of points below.

Exercise	% Body Weight		Resistance	Reps	% Rank	Strength Category	Pts
	Men	**Women**					
1. Lat Pull-Down	.70	.45					
2. Leg Extension	.65	.50					
3. Bench Press	.75	.45					
4. Curl-Up	.16	.10					
5. Leg Curl	.32	.25					
6. Arm Curl	.35	.18					
						Total Points	

Appendix C
Strength Training Record

Name _____ Age _____

Date					
Exercise	Wt Reps	Wt Reps	Wt Reps	Wt Reps	Wt Reps

Appendix C
Strength Training Record

Name _____ Age _____

Date					
Exercise	Wt Reps	Wt Reps	Wt Reps	Wt Reps	Wt Reps

Appendix C
Strength Training Record

Name _____ Age _____

Date					
Exercise	Wt Reps	Wt Reps	Wt Reps	Wt Reps	Wt Reps

Appendix C
Strength Training Record

Name _____ Age _____

Date					
Exercise	Wt Reps	Wt Reps	Wt Reps	Wt Reps	Wt Reps

Appendix D

Strength Training Worksheet

Name _____ Recovery _____

Body Part	Exercise	Sets	Reps	Resistance
Chest				
Midsection				
Triceps				
Legs				
Shoulders				
Neck				
Biceps				
Back				
Wrists				

Appendix D
Strength Training Worksheet

Name _____ Recovery _____

Body Part	Exercise	Sets	Reps	Resistance
Chest				
Midsection				
Triceps				
Legs				
Shoulders				
Neck				
Biceps				
Back				
Wrists				

Appendix D

Strength Training Worksheet

Name _____ Recovery _____

Body Part	Exercise	Sets	Reps	Resistance
Chest				
Midsection				
Triceps				
Legs				
Shoulders				
Neck				
Biceps				
Back				
Wrists				

Appendix D
Strength Training Worksheet

Name _____   Recovery _____

Body Part	Exercise	Sets	Reps	Resistance
Chest				
Midsection				
Triceps				
Legs				
Shoulders				
Neck				
Biceps				
Back				
Wrists				

Appendix E

Sports Training Worksheet

Name: _____

Sport: _____ Position: _____

Phase: _____ Intensity Cycle: ☐ Heavy / ☐ Light / ☐ # of Weeks ___

Core Exercises

Upper Body: _____

Lower Body: _____ Sets ___ / Reps ___ / Recovery _____

Total Body: _____ Resistance ___ % 1RM

Supplementary Exercises

Body Part   Exercise

_____   _____

_____   _____

_____   _____

_____   _____

_____   _____

_____   _____

_____   _____

_____   _____

_____   _____

Sets ___ / Reps ___ / Recovery _____

Resistance ___ % 1RM

Appendix E

Sports Training Worksheet

Name: _____

Sport: _____ Position: _____

Phase: _____ Intensity Cycle: ☐ Heavy / ☐ Light / ☐ # of Weeks ___

Core Exercises

Upper Body: _____

Lower Body: _____ Sets ___ / Reps ___ / Recovery _____

Total Body: _____ Resistance ___ % 1RM

Supplementary Exercises

Body Part   Exercise

_____ _____

_____ _____

_____ _____

_____ _____

_____ _____

_____ _____

_____ _____

_____ _____

_____ _____

_____ _____

Sets ___ / Reps ___ / Recovery _____

Resistance ___ % 1RM

Appendix E
Sports Training Worksheet

Name: _____

Sport: _____   Position: _____

Phase: _____   Intensity Cycle: ☐ Heavy / ☐ Light / ☐ # of Weeks ___

Core Exercises

Upper Body: _____

Lower Body: _____   Sets ___ / Reps ___ / Recovery _____

Total Body: _____   Resistance ___ % 1RM

Supplementary Exercises

Body Part   Exercise

_____   _____

_____   _____

_____   _____

_____   _____

_____   _____

_____   _____

_____   _____

_____   _____

_____   _____

_____   _____

Sets ___ / Reps ___ / Recovery _____

Resistance ___ % 1RM

Appendix E
Sports Training Worksheet

Name: _____

Sport: _____   Position: _____

Phase: _____   Intensity Cycle: ☐ Heavy / ☐ Light / ☐ # of Weeks ___

Core Exercises

Upper Body: _____

Lower Body: _____   Sets ___ / Reps ___ / Recovery _____

Total Body: _____   Resistance ___ % 1RM

Supplementary Exercises

Body Part   Exercise

_____   _____

_____   _____

_____   _____

_____   _____

_____   _____

_____   _____

_____   _____

_____   _____

_____   _____

_____   _____

Sets ___ / Reps ___ / Recovery _____

Resistance ___ % 1RM

Appendix F

Modified Periodization Worksheet

Name: _____

Sports: _____

Positions: _____

In-Season ☐   Off-Season ☐

Core Exercises

Five-set Day: 3 sets × 4 reps at 80% 1 RM
                2 sets × 2 reps at 90% 1 RM
Three-set Day: 2 sets × 4 reps at 80% 1 RM
                1 set × 2 reps at 90% 1 RM

Recovery Time: _____

Exercise	1 RM	80% 1 RM	90% 1 RM

Supplementary Exercises

Exercise	Sets	Reps	Recovery	Resistance

Appendix F

Modified Periodization Worksheet

Name: _____

Sports: _____

Positions: _____

In-Season ☐   Off-Season ☐

Core Exercises

Five-set Day: 3 sets × 4 reps at 80% 1 RM
                2 sets × 2 reps at 90% 1 RM
Three-set Day: 2 sets × 4 reps at 80% 1 RM
                1 sct × 2 rcps at 90% 1 RM

Recovery Time: _____

Exercise	1 RM	80% 1 RM	90% 1 RM

Supplementary Exercises

Exercise	Sets	Reps	Recovery	Resistance

Appendix F

Modified Periodization Worksheet

Name: _____

Sports: _____

Positions: _____

In-Season ☐   Off-Season ☐

Core Exercises

Five-set Day: 3 sets × 4 reps at 80% 1 RM
                     2 sets × 2 reps at 90% 1 RM
Three-set Day: 2 sets × 4 reps at 80% 1 RM
                     1 set × 2 reps at 90% 1 RM

Recovery Time: _____

Exercise	1 RM	80% 1 RM	90% 1 RM

Supplementary Exercises

Exercise	Sets	Reps	Recovery	Resistance

Appendix F
Modified Periodization Worksheet

Name: _____

Sports: _____

Positions: _____

In-Season ☐　　Off-Season ☐

Core Exercises

Five-set Day:　3 sets × 4 reps at 80% 1 RM
　　　　　　　　2 sets × 2 reps at 90% 1 RM
Three-set Day:　2 sets × 4 reps at 80% 1 RM
　　　　　　　　1 set × 2 reps at 90% 1 RM

Recovery Time: _____

Exercise	1 RM	80% 1 RM	90% 1 RM

Supplementary Exercises

Exercise	Sets	Reps	Recovery	Resistance

Appendix G

Nebraska Athletic Test

Name: _____

Ten-yard dash	Time: _____
Forty-yard dash	Time: _____
Twenty-yard shuttle run	Time: _____
Vertical Jump	Height: _____

Shuttle Run

Procedure: Draw two lines parallel to and five yards on either side of a center line. Begin the test in a three-point stance straddling the center line. The person timing starts the stopwatch with the first movement. The athlete then turns and runs either right or left to an outer line; touches the surface beyond the line; then reverses direction and runs and touches the surface beyond the other outside line; reverses direction again and finishes by crossing the center line.

Vertical Jump

Procedure: Stand facing the measuring board with the dominant arm fully extended and hold a piece of chalk in the hand to mark the height. The athlete then goes to a squat position with the feet flat on the floor. The athlete then jumps as high as possible and touches the measuring board with the chalk at the height of the jump. The vertical jump score is the difference between the first and second chalk marks.

Appendix G
Nebraska Athletic Test

Name: _____

Ten-yard dash	Time: _____
Forty-yard dash	Time: _____
Twenty-yard shuttle run	Time: _____
Vertical Jump	Height: _____

Shuttle Run

Procedure: Draw two lines parallel to and five yards on either side of a center line. Begin the test in a three-point stance straddling the center line. The person timing starts the stopwatch with the first movement. The athlete then turns and runs either right or left to an outer line; touches the surface beyond the line; then reverses direction and runs and touches the surface beyond the other outside line; reverses direction again and finishes by crossing the center line.

Vertical Jump

Procedure: Stand facing the measuring board with the dominant arm fully extended and hold a piece of chalk in the hand to mark the height. The athlete then goes to a squat position with the feet flat on the floor. The athlete then jumps as high as possible and touches the measuring board with the chalk at the height of the jump. The vertical jump score is the difference between the first and second chalk marks.

Appendix G

Nebraska Athletic Test

Name: _____

Ten-yard dash	Time:	_____
Forty-yard dash	Time:	_____
Twenty-yard shuttle run	Time:	_____
Vertical Jump	Height:	_____

Shuttle Run

Procedure: Draw two lines parallel to and five yards on either side of a center line. Begin the test in a three-point stance straddling the center line. The person timing starts the stopwatch with the first movement. The athlete then turns and runs either right or left to an outer line; touches the surface beyond the line; then reverses direction and runs and touches the surface beyond the other outside line; reverses direction again and finishes by crossing the center line.

Vertical Jump

Procedure: Stand facing the measuring board with the dominant arm fully extended and hold a piece of chalk in the hand to mark the height. The athlete then goes to a squat position with the feet flat on the floor. The athlete then jumps as high as possible and touches the measuring board with the chalk at the height of the jump. The vertical jump score is the difference between the first and second chalk marks.

Appendix G

Nebraska Athletic Test

Name: _____

Ten-yard dash	Time:	_____
Forty-yard dash	Time:	_____
Twenty-yard shuttle run	Time:	_____
Vertical Jump	Height:	_____

Shuttle Run

Procedure: Draw two lines parallel to and five yards on either side of a center line. Begin the test in a three-point stance straddling the center line. The person timing starts the stopwatch with the first movement. The athlete then turns and runs either right or left to an outer line; touches the surface beyond the line; then reverses direction and runs and touches the surface beyond the other outside line; reverses direction again and finishes by crossing the center line.

Vertical Jump

Procedure: Stand facing the measuring board with the dominant arm fully extended and hold a piece of chalk in the hand to mark the height. The athlete then goes to a squat position with the feet flat on the floor. The athlete then jumps as high as possible and touches the measuring board with the chalk at the height of the jump. The vertical jump score is the difference between the first and second chalk marks.

Appendix H

Bodybuilding Training Worksheet

Name _____ Recovery _____

Body Part	Exercise	Sets	Reps	Resistance
Chest				
Midsection				
Triceps				
Legs				
Shoulders				
Neck				
Biceps				
Back				
Wrists				

Appendix H
Bodybuilding Training Worksheet

Name _____ Recovery _____

Body Part	Exercise	Sets	Reps	Resistance
Chest				
Midsection				
Triceps				
Legs				
Shoulders				
Neck				
Biceps				
Back				
Wrists				

Appendix H
Bodybuilding Training Worksheet

Name _____ Recovery _____

Body Part	Exercise	Sets	Reps	Resistance
Chest				
Midsection				
Triceps				
Legs				
Shoulders				
Neck				
Biceps				
Back				
Wrists				

Appendix I

Periodicals on Strength Training

American Health and Fitness
Canusa Products, Inc.
2025 McKinley Street
Hollywood, FL 33020

Bigger, Faster, Stronger
BFS Publishing, Inc.
805 West 2400 South
Salt Lake City, UT 84119

Exercise and Health
Harris Publications, Inc.
1115 Broadway
New York, NY 10010

Flex
Weider Publications, Inc.
2100 Erwin Street
Woodland Hills, CA 91367

Ironman
Ironman Press
1701 Ives Avenue
Oxnard, CA 93033

Journal of Strength and Conditioning Research
National Strength and Conditioning Association
1955 North Union Boulevard
Colorado Springs, CO 80905

Men's Fitness
Weider Publications, Inc.
2100 Erwin Street
Woodland Hills, CA 91367

Muscle and Fitness
Weider Publications, Inc.
2100 Erwin Street
Woodland Hills, CA 91367

Muscle Media
Muscle Media Publishing, Inc.
555 Corporate Circle
Golden, CO 80401

Strength and Conditioning Journal
National Strength and Conditioning Association
1955 North Union Boulevard
Colorado Springs, CO 80905

Training and Conditioning
MAG, Inc.
2488 North Triphammer Road
Ithaca, NY 14850

Women's Physique World
Women's Physique World, Inc.
P.O. Box 429
Midland Park, NJ 07432

Bibliography

Allsen, Philip E., Joyce M. Harrison, and Barbara Vance. *Fitness for Life: An Individualized Approach.* 6th ed. Madison Wis.: McGraw-Hill, 1997.

American College of Sports Medicine. "Position Stand on Progression Models in Resistance Training for Healthy Adults." *Medicine and Science in Sports* 34, no. 2 (2002): 364–80.

———. "Position Statement on the Use and Abuse of Anabolic-Androgenic Steroids in Sport." *Medicine and Science in Sports* 19, no. 5 (1987): 534–39.

Baechle, Thomas R., and Roger W. Earle, eds. *Essentials of Strength Training and Conditioning.* 2^d ed. Champaign, Ill.: Human Kinetics, 2000.

Bompa, Tudor O. *Periodization of Strength.* Toronto, Ontario, Canada: Veritas, 1993.

Delavier, Frederic. *Strength Training Anatomy.* Champaign, Ill.: Human Kinetics, 2001.

Hatfield, Frederick C., and March L. Krotee. *Personalized Weight Training for Fitness and Athletics: From Theory to Practice.* 2^d ed. Dubuque, Iowa: Kendall/Hunt, 1994.

Hesson, James L. *Weight Training for Life.* 7th ed. Belmont, CA 2005.

Manore, Melinda and Janice Thompson. *Sports Nutrition for Health and Performance.* Champaign, Ill.: Human Kinetics, 2000.

McComas, Alan J. *Skeletal Muscle: Form and Function.* Champaign, Ill.: Human Kinetics, 1996.

Shepard, Greg. *Bigger, Faster, Stronger.* Champaign, Ill.: Human Kinetics, 2004.

Sienna, Phillip A. *One Rep Max: A Guide to Beginning Weight Training.* Madison, Wis.: Brown and Benchmark, 1989.

Wescott, Wayne. *Be Strong: Strength Training for Muscular Fitness for Men and Women.* Madison, Wis.: Brown and Benchmark, 1993.

Williams, Melvin H. *Nutrition for Fitness and Sport.* 4th ed. Madison, Wis.: Brown and Benchmark, 1995.

Index